Feel It Real!

Feel It Real!

A Guided Approach to Bringing the Law of Attraction into Your Life

DENISE COATES

ATRIA BOOKS

New York London Toronto Sydney

ATRIA BOOKS

A Division of Simon & Schuster, Inc.
1230 Avenue of the Americas
New York, NY 10020

First Atria Books hardcover edition June 2008

ATRIA BOOKS and colophon are trademarks of Simon & Schuster, Inc.

For information about special discounts for bulk purchases,
please contact Simon & Schuster Special Sales at
1-800-456-6798 or business@simonandschuster.com.

Designed by Dana Sloan

Manufactured in the United States of America

1 3 5 7 9 10 8 6 4 2

ISBN-13: 978-1-4165-6742-4
ISBN-10:   1-4165-6742-9

*This is dedicated to my wonderful clients
who inspired me to write this book*

The best and most beautiful things in the world

cannot be seen or even touched—they must be

felt with the heart.

HELEN KELLER

Contents

Section One

THE ART OF FEELING IT REAL

Section Two

A BOOK OF GAMES TO ATTRACT YOUR DESIRES

Games to Create a Life You Love

Games to Create Abundance and Wealth

Games to Create Your Ideal Body

Games to Create Career Success

Games to Create Objects / Things You Desire

Games to Create More Self-Love

CONTENTS

Acknowledgments

I am thankful to my clients for opening their hearts and minds and for urging me to write this book. Thanks to Abraham Hicks (www.abraham-hicks.com) for such clear teachings on the Law of Attraction. Thanks to my family for your support. Ram Dass, thank you for speaking directly to my Soul and encouraging me to do the same. Thanks with all my heart to Maharaj-ji (Neem Karoli Baba) for Being Love. Thanks to Angela for being my guide. Thanks to Regina, Holly, and the "Rabs" for your support and love, to the "Firbees" for your willingness to play with these games. To Connee for your enthusiastic support. Thanks to Zorro for gracing me with your companionship all these years. Thanks to Daisy, Bella, and Timmy for the pure, unadulterated joy you bring to my life. Also, eternal gratitude for my dear friend and fabulous PR/manager/support person, Macha Einbender. You felt it real with me all the way.

A big thanks to Amy Tannenbaum, my editor, for your brilliant suggestions and your faith in the book's ability to help others. Thanks also to Andrea Barzvi for all your support. Finally, I'd like to thank my husband and best friend, Andrew Smith, for all you did to help make this happen. My life began the day we met.

Introduction

For the longest time, I wasn't getting what I wanted from life. I was broke, in debt, unhealthy, in an unhappy relationship, and depressed. So who am I to be writing a book about how to get what you want from life?

A number of years ago, I discovered tools for living that are so easy, so powerful, and so consistent that my life became a total success almost overnight. My finances improved 10,000 percent, and my health problems disappeared. Not just one, but two dream careers flourished. I met and married the man of my dreams, bought my dream house, improved my relationships, and attracted a loving, spiritual community. I wrote, directed, and starred in a feature film bought by a wonderful distributor. Most important, I learned how to feel joy at will and to share that joy with others.

The tools I've discovered are based on a natural law of the Universe: the Law of Attraction. *Feel It Real!* is grounded on its powerful principle: everything draws to itself that which is like itself. Put another way, like attracts like.

This simple principle may be the most valuable law you'll learn for creating the life you want. This book discusses the Law of Attraction at length and gives you practical ways to apply it to your own life.

As a manifesting coach, I've taught hundreds of clients techniques I've devised based on the Law of Attraction. I am a firm believer in getting tangible, positive outcomes from working with spiritual principles, yet too often clients understand the theory behind making their lives better but don't have a clue about how to effectively apply it to their lives. To help them get fast results, I created practical games that provide positive outcomes. I sent clients daily lessons with games to simply attract their desires. As a trained clairvoyant and healer, I understood how people become mentally blocked against reaching their goals, and how to help them unblock their resistance to creating the lives they loved. Since many clients were blocked in similar areas, I devised games to address common issues, like money worries or feelings of unworthiness. I called them "games" instead of "exercises" because I wanted to remind them to have fun with the Law of Attraction, since being relaxed sends out a vibrational signal that makes playing the games more effective.

Soon clients were requesting a book based on these games, and this "how-to" manual was conceived. Over a three-year period, I honed the easily manageable steps in these games and infused my fifteen years of experience into them.

What can you expect from this book? A lot. This book offers the simple "rules" for creating your desired life and an easy, step-by-step approach for applying them. If you use the games consistently, you will experience immediate and long-term positive benefits. You will learn to manifest your deepest desires.

I want to help as many people as possible grasp these simple techniques for manifesting their desires. My experience with hundreds of clients has shown that people who are ready to improve their lives and set their clear intentions will achieve their desires. It's as simple as that. It works if you work it.

Don't just read this book—apply it. If you only read the book, you will understand how the Power of the Universe can deliver your desires, but you won't be using that power. Practicing these games will change your life, your moods will lift, and you will attract what you want.

So let's get started. All you need to bring to the table is an open mind, a little willingness, and a desire to improve your life. Let's start with an intention. List all the things you want to get out of this book. Go for it. Pretend it's your birthday and you can have anything you want.

HELPFUL HINT: Imagine you've just read the last page of this book after practicing all of the games. What do you want to have accomplished, understood, and applied? How do you want to feel as you're closing the book?

From reading *Feel It Real!* I intend to get the following results:

_____

_____

_____

_____

You just acted in a powerful way. You've given the Universe a clear command to bring you your desired results. When you finish this book, go back and reread this intention. You might be amazed at how the Universe has delivered.

How to Use This Book

L ike vibrational sheet music, this book is intended to help you hit and hold the vibrational notes essential for manifesting your desires. Scientists agree that all matter in the Universe is made up of energy, including human beings. Though we appear solid to the human eye, we are not. Reduced down to our smallest components, we humans are made up of nothing more than energetic vibrations. What's more, how we're feeling and what we're thinking influence how we as energy are vibrating. Scientists are coming to the conclusion that even our thoughts and emotions are made up of energy. Our thoughts and emotions are things and are as physically tangible as our legs or our hair. If we could see ourselves at an energetic level, we would see that we are constantly sending out vibrational signals in the form of thoughts and feelings. According to the Law of Attraction, vibrational frequencies attract similar frequencies to themselves.

The thoughts we choose to think and the feelings we choose to feel become extremely important because they attract matching vibrations back to us in the form of more thoughts, feelings, and circumstances. So hitting these emotional notes will attract back matching experiences in our lives. The more we "hold the note" of abundance, the more abundance will reflect back to us from our physical universe. As we learn to hold the note of success, the more outer success and unconditional love we will experience and the better our relationships will become.

Before you start, get a journal or a spiral notebook in which you can write your responses to the questions and games in the book. Although there are sample spaces provided, these may not offer you enough space to write all of your thoughts. Call it your *Feel It Real!* journal. Also, use this journal to record all of your experiences with the games. In a few months you can look at your journal to see how far you've come and how many dreams have come true.

Remember, the exercises in this book are called "games" for a reason. The more fun you have with them, the more profound the manifestation process becomes. This may sound paradoxical, but I suggest you take feeling good seriously. This takes practice, since it goes against most of what we've been programmed to feel. It's time to get serious about not being so serious. As you learn to make these games more fun and less work, you will soften your resistance and allow in the well-being that is your birthright.

In the second section of this book, you will find a variety of specific games for raising your frequency and attracting your desires. Work with the games that feel good to you in the moment. What feels good changes from day to day, so browse through the games section and settle on one that fits what you're looking for. Some games focus on creating your life the way you envision it. Some are specific to manifesting particular desires. And some games are for quickly raising your vibration when you want to feel more positive but don't have a lot of time. If you sense some resistance when playing a certain game, try a different game and come back to the initial one later. Use this like a recipe book. Decide from day to day which recipe sounds the most delicious. Your *Feel It Real!* journal will allow you to reflect on the games most helpful to you.

I have included a final section called "My Wins," where you can take note of what desires, big and small, have manifested along the way. Too often we gloss over the great things we are creating because we're so focused on what's not here yet. By writing down your successes, you will attract more. Noting them also reinforces your faith in yourself and in the Law of Attraction. Also, by reading your wins aloud on a daily basis, you will consistently be sending out vibrations of success and gratitude, which, in turn, attracts into your life more success and more reasons to feel grateful.

Remember, though, to make the main goal of the games to experience good feelings, not merely to focus on manifestations. If you approach these games with the intent of enjoying the moment, then the manifestations will take care of themselves. So make the following commitment to yourself:

I _____ plan to use these games in order to feel good and have fun. I acknowledge that my main purpose for playing these games is for the sheer joy of it; the Law of Attraction will take care of the rest and deliver my desires to me in joyful and fun ways.

With this in mind, let's begin.

Section One

❖

The Art of
Feeling It Real

1

Why It's Good to Have Desires

Man's reach should exceed his grasp,
or what's a heaven for?

— ROBERT BROWNING

I am so pleased you have chosen this book as a means to express your true nature by learning to create all you desire. There is nothing wrong with desire. I repeat: there is nothing wrong with desire. In fact, everything is right about having and manifesting your desires. It is what keeps the Universe thriving. Desiring allows it to expand itself into more and more creations.

Each of you is a continuum of this energy that wishes to create and expand itself in new and adventurous ways. Think of history's pioneers: Columbus, Magellan, Leonardo da Vinci, Rosa Parks. All of these pioneers felt the desire to reach beyond what already existed and expand into a New World, whether it was discovering new lands, creating amazing inventions, or being a catalyst for civil liberties. We've explored our oceans and now continue to explore farther and farther into outer space. Just as these outer frontiers exist, so do the inner frontiers of our spirit, waiting for us to discover, uncover, and reveal them.

This eternal expansion is important for us to experience; this is why we're here on this big, blue planet. We've always been and always will be pioneers, eternally unfolding through the process of desire and manifestation.

Have you ever wondered where your desires come from? Do you sometimes feel as if they are choosing you rather than the other way around? Desire is part of life, and your desires desire you as much as you desire them. In metaphysical terms, you are matching frequencies with your desire, and your soul wants to manifest these desires to expand consciousness. Unfortunately, some preach that desires are a no-no and claim them to be the source of suffering. Have you ever seen children making sculptures with clay? Have you seen them finger painting or playing make-believe? They don't look like they're suffering to me. This is because their natural state is to be creative and full of desire. This doesn't change after we become adults. We may suppress our desires and our creativity, but we can never eliminate them because they are as natural to us as breathing.

Think about it this way. If no one had desires, the following things would not exist:

Sistine Chapel

airplanes

automobiles

medicine

babies

teachers

Mozart's music

your favorite books

your favorite movies

your favorite music

Earth itself and the Universe, for that matter

I want you to ask yourself some questions about the concept of desire. What were you taught? What are your beliefs about having desire? Is it good? Is it bad?

List below what you believe about having desires. Right or wrong? Suffering or joy? Something to embrace or overcome?

_____

_____

_____

_____

_____

_____

_____

_____

Before you play these games, it's important to give yourself absolute permission to have desires. Say the following affirmation if ever you doubt yourself about having desires: "Desire is a form of Love."

You may ask, "What about destructive desires that come from addictions? Is that a form of love?"

Let this be your meter to know which desires are appropriate:

AS LONG AS IT DOES NOT HARM YOURSELF

OR OTHERS TO HAVE THE DESIRE,

THEN IT IS OF LOVE.

Addictions and destructive urges are actually not desires. They are means of escaping from your true feelings. It is necessary to have authentic feelings in order for true desires to be born. When people spend the majority of their time numbing their authentic feelings with addictions, their inner guidance system can't access their true desires. True desires uplift and are helpful to the individual and to others. True desires feel good in a wholesome, healthy way. True desires are beautiful in the light of day.

One more important note about desires: many times clients have come to me desiring a specific person into or back into his/her life. But that person is clearly not interested in him/her romantically, or is with someone else, or is unloving. In this case, when my client asks if it's good to hold a desire for a specific person, I say, "You are limiting the Universe by telling it who

6

would be the truest love for you. Tell the Universe that you want to feel in love, how you want to be treated, and how you want to treat the other. Then let the Universe work out the details of who it is and how they will come into your life." In this and in many other situations, it's best to describe how you want to feel, but not outline how that feeling should be manifested.

You'll know which desires are good for you by how they make you feel. If thinking about them makes you feel joyful, light, connected, and happy, and if they are not harmful to another, then your emotional guidance system is signaling that these desires are born of love.

2

Law of Attraction

You are a living magnet. What you attract into your
life is in harmony with your dominant thoughts.

— BRIAN TRACY

Law of Attraction is a cosmic law governing the Universe.
It says that like frequencies attract like frequencies. What
does this law have to do with manifesting your desires?

Everything.

In human terms, this law translates into: you get more of whatever you are focusing on because, as you focus, you vibrate at a certain
frequency that attracts anything vibrating at the same frequency.

You've heard the expression "When it rains, it pours." This
makes sense from the standpoint of the Law of Attraction,
because it's essentially saying that when you focus on how much
it is raining, it will rain even more. Or take Murphy's Law,
which states: "If anything can go wrong, it will." This is because
focusing on things not going well attracts the frequency that

9

manifests things getting worse. You can apply the Law of Attraction to many statements. Consider these:

Now that I'm looking for it, I'm seeing it everywhere.
The more I give, the more I get.
The rich get richer, the poor get poorer.
Birds of a feather flock together.

So many self-help books set out to teach people that thinking positive thoughts, speaking positive words, and doing positive things will give them positive results. But little attention is placed on the importance of having positive feelings. Our feelings are our signals telling us if the thoughts we send out as vibratory frequencies attract what we want, or what we don't want.

We create with our thoughts and emotions. When emotions are added to thought, they create what I call "emotional thought" and speed up the delivery of focused desires. When we feel good, our emotions speed up the magnetization of the thought signals we are sending out.

Talk about an elaborate creational device! We've been taught to believe we are at the mercy of our feelings and we should fear them, or even worse, ignore them. On the contrary, not only is it safe to listen to our emotions, but it's also absolutely necessary to, if we intend to attract our desires. Not listening to both positive and negative emotions is like walking around in a power outage without a flashlight. Until we learn to listen to our emotions and train ourselves to feel better by refocusing our thoughts and feelings, our lives will be a haphazard set of circumstances.

As we learn to feel or "vibrate" at higher frequencies that correspond to joy, abundance, happiness, gratitude, awe, wonder, appreciation, and love, we will know our thoughts are beginning to attract circumstances back to us that match these higher frequencies. Therefore, the Law of Attraction works in our favor. The more grateful we feel, the more things we receive to feel grateful for. The more loved we feel, the more love we receive. The more beautiful we feel, the more attractive we become.

Let's forget about the concept that thoughts alone change our lives. I can say positive affirmations all day long, but if I'm not feeling them, I will get little from the experience. Let's forget about the concept that hard work alone is what's going to change our lives. We can work to the point of exhaustion (as most of us have) trying to get a better life, but without feeling good first, this method takes too much effort for too little reward. Instead, we will charge our thoughts with positive emotions in order to feel better, and then watch the magic unfold in a seemingly effortless dance. Life wasn't meant to be hard. You're not here to suffer in order to learn. We've all suffered enough for ten thousand lifetimes, and we don't seem to be learning all that much from it. Why not make a decision today to learn from joy? More than coming to this glorious planet to learn, we came to create joy. Joy begets joy begets joy. Like frequencies attract like frequencies.

So let's get attracting.

Understanding the Law of Attraction

Think of a time in your life when you expected the worst, felt negative, and then seemed to attract more bad things.

EXAMPLE

On my first day of work, I was worried about getting there on time. I got stuck in a huge traffic jam and ended up being late. Now your turn. (Remember to use your journal if you need more space.)

_____

_____

_____

_____

Now think of a time in your life where you expected the best, felt good, and from that seemed to attract more good things.

EXAMPLE

The same week I started volunteering at the local food bank, I got an unexpected raise at work. Your turn:

_____

_____

_____

_____

Now that you understand how the Law of Attraction works, let me help you to use it in your life, right at this moment.

Learning How to Feel It First

The first thing is to get clear on what you want to manifest. Pick any one desire. (We'll be working on many in this book, but let's focus on just one for this exercise.) What emotions would you experience if you already had this thing in your life? List as many emotions as possible.

EXAMPLE

"I want to be financially wealthy." The emotions you might have if you were already financially wealthy:

1. comfortable
2. relieved
3. grateful
4. prosperous
5. relaxed
6. joyful
7. peaceful
8. generous
9. luxurious
10. safe

Now your turn:

One thing I'm wanting to manifest in my life right now is:

_____

_____

_____

_____

The emotions I would feel if I already had this are:

1._____

2._____

3._____

4._____

5._____

6._____

7._____

8._____

9._____

10._____

We have been taught that once we get the thing we want, we can give ourselves permission to feel good feelings. If we want to learn how to manifest the lives we envision, we'll want to feel the happy feelings first, then watch the miracles unfold in our lives. The "cart before the horse" in this case is hoping that getting the desire will make us feel good. The truth is that feeling good is what brings the desire.

As I learned about the Law of Attraction in my own life, I decided to practice feeling wealthy when I was still broke, feeling thin when I was still overweight, feeling successful in my career before I was successful, and feeling deeply in love when I was still single. It took a bit to get the hang of this, because the old negative-feeling habits were so ingrained, and "reality" was saying that those things weren't here yet . . . so why should I be happy? The big shift happened for me when I realized that the only reason I wanted my goals was to feel the feelings I thought I would have if I had my desires. If I could figure out a way to feel those positive feelings even before the desires appeared, that was all that mattered. I learned to go right for the feelings I thought having my goals would give me, not caring so much about the outcomes. Paradoxically, it was only when I cared more about the feelings than the results that my manifesting really took off.

When you work with the Law of Attraction, you will realize that the people you consider to be "lucky" are consciously (or unconsciously) using the law. In any area in which they are successful, they feel good before the good gets here. You may ask these people how they became successful, and every one of them will admit to feeling that they "knew" it was going to happen for them. They imagined how it would feel to have it, and it came to them. They became so experienced at feeling good about their desire before they manifested it that, by law, the Universe had to yield their desire to them.

One of the biggest determining factors regarding whether someone knows their desires are going to manifest or not has to do with their beliefs. Those who believe that they will win usually do. Those who believe that "feeling it first" works prove themselves right. Our beliefs largely determine what we're even willing to think about. Thus, deliberately choosing empowering beliefs is of the utmost importance in using the Law of Attraction.

You've heard it a million times from well-meaning people: "Change your beliefs." "Have a little faith." "What you believe, you can achieve." If it were so easy to shift our beliefs to create perfect lives, everyone would be in ideal surroundings. Although we know that changing our beliefs would change our lives, most of us only have a vague idea of why and are clueless as to how to go about changing them.

Working with my clients over the years I have become a "belief researcher," studying the "why" of beliefs and how to change them. Though I still have much to learn, I've made some big headway in the area of *how* to change our beliefs easily and painlessly. I've discovered that we can use the Law of Attraction to create *anything* we desire, including more empowering beliefs. How do we attract more positively magnetic beliefs? You guessed it! By getting into the feeling place of already having empowering beliefs.

But first, let's look at how our beliefs are currently affecting our overall vibration. I will list some oppositional beliefs, and you decide if they raise or lower your vibrational frequencies. Ready?

"Money doesn't grow on trees."

OR

"Money flows to me easily."

Which one felt better emotionally? How about these:

"People you love will leave you."

OR

"The ones you love will always be there for you."

"It takes hard work to achieve your goals."

OR

"When I follow my passion, money flows effortlessly into my life."

"Everything I eat goes right to my waist."

OR

"I have a high metabolism and stay thin eating whatever I want."

Our beliefs are directly affecting our emotional signals and therefore what we are attracting. Using the Law of Attraction becomes most powerful once we've identified which negative beliefs we are sending out into the Universe, because we can then change them to the positive. We'll talk more about beliefs later, but I've introduced the power of beliefs here because it is important for you to understand that some people won't truly commit to playing the games in this book or working with the Law of Attraction because of their limiting beliefs, which tell them "This attracting business isn't real" or "Feeling it real works for everyone but me." And, as a result, the Law of Attraction will bring you circumstances that reflect your limiting beliefs. So if you find yourself avoiding playing these games, you might ask yourself what beliefs you have that are holding you back from creating a life you love.

Before we proceed, I want to share a basic formula for using the Law of Attraction, based on what we've discussed thus far. All the games in this book are creative variations on this basic formula.

1. State your desire.
2. Ask yourself what feelings you might have if you already had that desire.
3. Get into the feeling place of already having that desire.
4. Stay in the feeling place of already having the desire for as long as possible each day.
5. Decide that imagining these good feelings is its own reward, knowing that as you enjoy the feelings for their own sake, the Universe will deliver your desires to you by Law of Attraction.

Now that we understand what the Law of Attraction is and have the basic formula for creating, let's talk a bit about "Reality" and how changeable it truly is.

3

What Is Reality, Really?

Reality is merely an illusion,
albeit a very persistent one.

— ALBERT EINSTEIN

If it's this easy, why isn't everyone living the life of their dreams? The biggest obstacle to "feeling it real" is that we have been taught since birth to observe "what is" more than we have been taught to imagine what we'd like it to be. We think everything we see around us is the cause of our feelings and thoughts. In truth, everything we see in our lives is the result of our great imaginations. All of our current circumstances are a result or an effect of previous thoughts and emotions. Think about it. Everything was once just a thought or an idea. Everything that exists first began as an idea. To understand this better, let's do the following.

What Really Is Reality?

Look around you right now and write down the first three things you set your eyes on.

EXAMPLE

> my phone
>
> a painting on the wall
>
> a ring on my finger

Three things I'm looking at right now:

_____

_____

_____

For each item, decide if it existed throughout eternity or if at some point it was just an idea. Write down whose idea it was.

EXAMPLE

> 1. My phone came from Alexander Graham Bell.
> 2. The painting came from Gustav Klimt.
> 3. The ring came from a jewelry maker.

Now your turn:

1._____

2._____

3._____

You might ask, "What if I'm looking at a tree or a dog or a star?" We'll discuss this later in the book, but I'm a firm believer that such elaborately detailed designs came from some Intelligent Source.

Why do we turn these outer circumstances into our "reality"? The nature of our checkbooks makes us vibrate at wealth or poverty. The mood of a spouse determines if we will vibrate at lovable or unlovable. It's crazy, really. From watching the news, we might determine that the world is going to hell in a handbasket, yet crime has declined each year for the past several years.

Isn't reality always changing? Are you in the same circumstances that you were in ten years ago, one year ago, or even a week ago? Once we stop honoring "what is" as the be-all and end-all of reality, we are free to focus on our imaginations and their resulting emotional frequencies. These thoughts and ideas will eventually manifest into solid realities.

Many of us feel that the movies of our lives are set in stone—they're unchangeable. In truth, we are the writers and directors of our movies. If we choose to focus on appreciative thoughts, visualizations of a happier future, and our fondest memories, we will begin to vibrate at a different wavelength. We would begin to attract a New Reality that is still changeable but akin to our desires. The message is: stop reacting and start imagining.

How do we learn to extricate ourselves from this dogmatic belief that everything we see is real? The first step is to focus only on the parts of our current "reality" that we like and want to continue attracting, all those elements that you are happy with. Make a list of these things.

More, Please!

EXAMPLE

In my present life, I am currently happy with: my dogs, my car, my husband, my relationship with my friend Janie, my mother, and the weather in my city.

Now your turn:

In my present life, I am currently happy with (list *all* of the things you can think of, big and little):

_____

_____

_____

_____

_____

This exercise more than likely raised your frequencies, because focusing on what you do like is a giant frequency raiser.

Continue to focus on the aspects of your current reality that you're already happy with. As you focus your appreciation on them, by the Law of Attraction, they will get better and better and you will have much more to be happy about. *Like attracts like*. If you are appreciating all the good in your life now, guess what—you're going to attract more just like it.

For fun, go over your list and say a "thank-you" out loud to each thing in your life with which you are currently happy.

For instance: "Thank you, car." "Thank you, Janie." "Thank you, great weather." This may be the first time you've actively acknowledged what is working in your life. The Universe *loves* when you acknowledge the good you already have.

If you're thinking, "There is nothing I am happy about in my life right now," I want you to dig a little deeper. If you have the capability to read this book, I am already aware of many things you might have to be happy about. You have your eyesight. You live in a country that allows you to read whatever you choose. You had the money to buy the book or someone gave it to you, which means someone cares. You get it? There are always many things we can be happy about in our lives right now. As we learn to appreciate what good is already here, we will, by law, begin to attract more of the same.

Your next question is, "What about the parts I don't like?" Well, on to the next chapter.

4

Opposites Create Desires

Out of difficulties grow miracles.

—JEAN DE LA BRUYÈRE

Our world is composed of opposites. There's no light without darkness, no cold without hot. There's love and hate, wet and dry, rich and poor, up and down, in and out. What does this have to do with attracting your good? Again . . .

Everything!

Opposites create desires. If not for opposites, we would have no contrast, no way to differentiate anything from anything else—and no need to desire anything. Without poverty, sickness, loneliness, and fear, we wouldn't be able to summon the desire for wealth, health, connection, and safety. The world would be without relativity, without differences. So let's praise opposites. Let's celebrate negative emotions and conditions, for without them, we wouldn't be able to summon the clarity that comes from having a desire born from exposure to its opposite.

The Universe was designed to have opposites. As we discussed in chapter 1, this is why we came here to this planet of opposites—for the sheer joy of desiring and creating!

Any subject you focus on also involves considering its opposite. When you focus with feeling on something you don't want, you get more of it, but when you focus positive feelings on what you do want, you get more of that. Let's play "the opposite game" to attract the things we *do* want.

That's right, we'll flip around the thing we're not enjoying in our present to an image/thought/emotion/creation of the thing's opposite.

The Opposite Game

List all the things in your life that you aren't happy with. (Now you get to gripe.)

EXAMPLE

In my present life I am currently unhappy with: my finances, my weight, my health, my career, my friendships and my self-esteem.

Now your turn. In my present life I am currently unhappy with (list *all* you can think of, big and little):

_____

_____

_____

_____

In order to find their opposite, we need to identify how these "Unhappys" make us feel. Write out your first three "Unhappys," then write the negative feelings you feel from them.

EXAMPLE

1. I'm unhappy with my weight. This makes me feel: *unconfident, ugly, ashamed, invisible.*
2. I'm unhappy with my career. This makes me feel: *stuck, unlucky, jealous of others.*
3. I'm unhappy with my self-esteem. This makes me feel: *unconfident, alone, self-hating.*

Now your turn:

1. I'm unhappy with _____. This makes me feel:

_____

2. I'm unhappy with _____. This makes me feel:

_____

3. I'm unhappy with _____. This makes me feel:

_____

The purpose of the opposite game is to get you to feel or "vibrate" at the opposite emotions so you can start to attract opposite circumstances. Let's try it now.

EXAMPLE

(From above) I'm unhappy with my weight, from which I feel unconfident, ugly, ashamed, guilty and invisible.

What are the *opposite* emotions of these?

unconfident	becomes	*confident, self-assured, glowing*
ugly	becomes	*beautiful, gorgeous, shining*
ashamed	becomes	*self-accepting, compassionate toward self, self-forgiving*
invisible	becomes	*shining, glowing, bold, magnetic*

Now you do the opposite game with your three "Unhappys":

1. I'm unhappy with my _____, which makes me feel:

_____

_____

_____

_____

What are the *opposite* emotions of these?

_____ becomes _____

_____ becomes _____

_____ becomes _____

2. I'm unhappy with my _____, which makes me feel:

_____

_____

_____

_____

What are the *opposite* emotions of these?

_____ becomes _____

_____ becomes _____

_____ becomes _____

3. I'm unhappy with my _____, which makes me feel:

_____

_____

_____

_____

What are the *opposite* emotions of these?

_____ becomes _____

_____ becomes _____

_____ becomes _____

This list of opposite emotions is a road map for creating conditions different from the ones we've attracted so far.

How? By focusing as much time as possible on those opposite, positive emotions before our desires get here. Now let's play the opposite game in a new way. We will reverse the "nondesire" into a desire.

EXAMPLE

1. *I'm unhappy with my weight*   becomes   *I'm thin and attractive.*

2. *I'm unhappy with my career*   becomes   *I have a successful and joyous career.*

3. *I'm unhappy with*   becomes   *I have a great sense of self-*
   my self esteem   *confidence, self-love, and*
                                   self-esteem.

Now your turn:

1. I'm unhappy with my _____ becomes:

_____

_____

_____

2. I'm unhappy with my _____ becomes:

_____

_____

_____

3. I'm unhappy with my _____ becomes:

_____

_____

_____

Now that we have created both the wanted from the unwanted and the positive emotions from the negative emotions, we are on the way to changing our conditions.

You are now allowed to focus only on the *opposite feelings* of how these "Unhappys" make you feel. Take these three desires and make them part of your overall intention for what you want to accomplish by reading this book.

Write down the new desire and, next to it, the desired emotions (as we did above).

EXAMPLE

1. I'm thin and attractive.

   I feel confident, beautiful, self-accepting, self-loving, shining, glowing, sexy, flowing, changing, hopeful, excited.
2. I have a successful and joyous career.

   I feel growing, moving, lucky, loved, happy for others' success.

Go for it. (You will be referring to this list often, as we will be working with these three desires throughout the book.)

1. I am/have: _____

   I feel: _____

   _____

   _____

2. I am/have: _____

   I feel: _____

   _____

   _____

3. I am/have: _____

   I feel: _____

   _____

   _____

Now write this list out on a piece of paper, or tape-record it and read or listen to it twice a day—once in the morning and once at night. Now that you've played the opposite game, continue to focus only on what you like about your current "reality" and the opposite of what you don't like about your current reality. By focusing on those two aspects of your "reality," your entire world will change for the better.

5

Feeling It First

A strong passion will insure success, for the desire
of the end will point out the means.

— WILLIAM HAZLITT

Knowing what you don't want helped you figure out what you do want and how you want to feel. You might ask, "How do I feel that way before getting my desire?"

There are many processes and techniques that can help you create the feeling that you already possess the things you desire. The games in the book will help. Let's reiterate why it is so important to feel it first.

When you exist in a vibration of already having your desires, you begin to send a new signal to the Universe. The signal says, "Send me more stuff that matches the way I am feeling." The Universe always says yes to whatever emotional signal you send it by delivering circumstances that vibrationally match up with those emotions.

You get the green lights and the open doors more and more. Seemingly miraculous synchronicities begin to happen, all because you tuned in to a different "emotional station." This book is designed to get and keep you feeling as if you have your desires, even before they get here, and to help you become aware of beliefs that hold you back from the feeling place of having your desires.

Feeling It Real

Let's work with the three desires you listed (page 31) and help you get into the feeling place of already having them. Look at the positive emotions you've listed. Our goal is to get you to feel those emotions *right now*. These emotions are our navigational system or road map.

Take the emotions you want to feel from your first desire and think of any ways, even little ways, you *already* feel these emotions. You can combine similar emotions for the sake of keeping it relatively easy.

EXAMPLE

1. I am thin and attractive.
   I feel confident, beautiful, self-accepting, self-loving, shining, glowing, sexy, flowing, changing, hopeful, excited.
   I *already* feel confident when I am at work because I am good at what I do.

I *already* feel beautiful/sexy when I curl my hair.

I *already* feel self-accepting/self-loving when I am first waking up in the morning (before I've had a chance to beat up on myself).

Now it's your turn. Think of any ways you already feel the emotions that your delivered desires will cause. Remember you can combine similar emotions for the sake of keeping it easy.

1. I am/have _____

   I feel _____

   _____

   I *already* feel _____

   when _____

   _____

   I *already* feel _____

   when _____

   _____

   I *already* feel _____

   when _____

   _____

2. I am/have _____

   I feel _____

   _____

   I *already* feel _____

when _____

_____

I *already* feel _____

when _____

_____

I *already* feel _____

when _____

_____

3. I am/have _____

I feel _____

_____

I *already* feel _____

when _____

_____

I *already* feel _____

when _____

_____

I *already* feel _____

when _____

_____

It's clear that you've already experienced some version of these emotions. The more often you consciously choose to experience these emotions, the faster you will attract your desires.

Notice how you feel, now that you've spent so much time

focusing on the good in your life. There are certain physical/emotional/mental/spiritual sensations that we experience when we vibrationally or emotionally tune in to our desires. The common signs that you're raising frequencies and attracting your desires include:

1. Brighter eyes when you look in the mirror. (You are literally vibrating at a higher frequency, and more energy is pouring through your body.)
2. Feeling giddy, laughing, and being silly. This is a really common clue.
3. Feeling calm and peaceful deep in your core.
4. Feeling a comforting tingling or buzzing in your body, like a vibrational hug.
5. Feeling more energized and needing less sleep.
6. Feeling more loving and compassionate toward others.
7. Feeling a desire to have more fun.
8. Feeling that your five senses are more heightened.
9. Experiencing psychic visions/dreams/premonitions.
10. Feeling more inspired and guided in your decision making.
11. Noticing that others are more attracted to your energy, and want to be around you or talk to you on the phone more.

All of these experiences are clues that you're vibrating at higher frequencies and thus "feeling it first." You will want to familiarize yourself with these feelings, because they're the first piece of evidence that your desires are manifesting. When you begin to sense a heightened feeling of joy, even elation or bliss about your desire before it manifests, you are vibrationally aligned and are attracting it RIGHT NOW.

When you do these exercises, and in daily life, observe if you notice any of these changes (physical, emotional, spiritual) so you can identify when you are in the mode of attracting your desires. List the changes you notice:

_____

_____

_____

_____

_____

Now that we've learned about the Law of Attraction, changing our reality, opposites, and feeling it first, it is time to learn how our emotions and beliefs help, and sometimes hinder, our vibrational output and our ability to attain our desires.

6

The Magic of Emotions

The most certain sign of wisdom is continual
cheerfulness; her state is like the things above the
moon, always clear and serene.

— MICHEL DE MONTAIGNE

Understanding our emotional lives is important for creating the lives we love. Emotions are like an internal compass that constantly sends chemical messages and electrical currents through our physical bodies to let us know that what we are focusing on is either beneficial or unbeneficial to our lives. Our emotions reflect whatever it is we are currently thinking about or focusing on. When we focus on what we do want, we feel better emotionally. When we focus on what we don't want, we feel negative emotions.

Why are so many people afraid to listen to and feel their emotions? Perhaps letting down our emotional walls makes us feel out of control. Many of us have been taught to ignore, negate, belittle, and repress our emotions for so long that our lives have become a constant struggle to avoid our emotional guidance. The more we attempt to ignore our emotions, the more intense they become. The more intense they become, the more intimidated we become by their intensity. The more intimidated we become, the more we attempt to ignore them. And the cycle continues. It is easy to see how someone could become frightened if they think that the intensity of their emotions could somehow be dangerous.

Nothing could be further from the truth. If we learned to reassimilate our emotional lives back into our psyches, we would feel more integrated with mind and body, we'd free up so much more energy to experience the present moment without constantly guarding ourselves, and we would be better able to direct our emotions in creative ways, thus allowing us to better shape the course of our lives. When we know how we're feeling, we know how we're vibrating. When we know how we're vibrating, we know what we're attracting. The easiest way to change what we're attracting is to change what we're feeling, but we can't change how we're feeling until we *know* how we're feeling. Thus, cultivating a moment-to-moment awareness of our emotions is like noticing when our musical instrument is out of tune so that we may tune it. If we assume it's in tune or ignore that we are out of key, the "song" of our life suffers.

Emotional thoughts emit frequencies that radiate from us, and they attract anything similar back into our lives. For optimum mental health, it's important to make friends with our emotions. But what can be even more beneficial—once we reclaim our emotional selves and control our focus—is that we are then empowered to attract, by our emotional frequency, the lives we want.

Where do we begin? How about at the beginning?

Reclaiming Our Lost Emotions

To begin the process, we must identify our emotions and the associated frequencies that govern our experiences.

The following exercise will help you dig down deep to find the core emotions vibrating within you on a daily basis. Forget what you think is "likable" or "reasonable" and be real. The fact that you hide your emotions doesn't mean they aren't still vibrating and secretly running, and sometimes ruining, your life.

Be as honest as possible with this exercise. Try not to censor yourself about what are "acceptable" and "unacceptable" emotions.

Acknowledgment is the first step toward making friends with your emotions. Have you ever been hurt because a friend, potential lover, or fellow worker ignored you? It does hurt. In fact, most children would rather receive negative attention than no attention at all. One of our biggest fears is the fear of feeling invisible. Now is the time you can empathize with your emotional self. Such attention may be long overdue, because your emotional self has probably felt invisible for much of your life.

Complete the following exercise when you have several minutes to spare. Try to do it all at once, rather than in segments.

Meeting Your Disowned Emotional Self

Say the following questions out loud, then fill in the blanks with the first answer that comes to mind.

1. The emotions I am most afraid to express in my life are

_____

_____

_____

2. Growing up, it was never okay to feel _____

_____

_____

_____

3. I get really embarrassed when the emotion of _____

_____

_____

_____

_____ takes over.

4. When I was a child, I used to feel a lot more_____

_____

5. It seems to me that when I feel _____

_____, I get in a lot of trouble.

6. My mother rarely let(s) herself feel _____

7. My father rarely let(s) himself feel _____

8. If I knew no one would judge me for it, I would let myself
   feel _____

9. The emotion(s) I'm most likely to hide from others are

_____

_____

_____

10. The emotions I feel safe expressing are _____

_____

_____

_____

_____

11. I was encouraged to feel _____

_____

_____

_____

_____ as a child.

12. My mother seems(ed) to let herself feel _____

_____

_____

_____

13. My father seems(ed) to let himself feel _____

_____

_____

_____

14. I have been given the most approval in my life for feeling

_____

_____

_____

This exercise helps you to reclaim the ability to listen to your feelings and reestablish a solid relationship between you and your emotional guidance system so that, from this awareness, you may more deliberately pick and choose the emotional signals you want to send out to the Universe, thus attracting more desirable circumstances to you.

It's truly important to give yourself permission to feel all of your emotions. I once read an article about a girl who was diagnosed with a syndrome where she wasn't able to feel physical pain. You may think that would be a good thing, but her parents sure didn't. They or someone they trusted had to be with her 24/7 to make sure she didn't accidentally hurt herself and not know it.

This may sound extreme, but most of us live our whole lives numbed to what our emotions are trying to tell us. Our emotions were designed to guide us in the same way that physical pain and pleasure were designed to guide us—away from hurtful things and toward helpful things.

Emotions like anger, grief, frustration, and fear have important messages to give us. They signal that our thoughts aren't in alignment with our desires. Psychologists and scientists have verified that suppressing emotions over time can cause mental and physical illness.

As we allow ourselves to listen to our emotions, we are more able to deliberately choose our emotions. When we feel a negative emotion, we can look for the thought causing the emotion and shift it toward something that makes us feel better. This process can be done gradually, by feeling a little bit better at a time. We can go from rage to anger to a light frustration to humor about a situation by gently guiding ourselves toward happier thoughts.

Try the following:

A Little Bit Better Game

Pick a topic in your life that is causing you negative emotion. It could be something that causes you frustration, sadness, worry, etc.

EXAMPLE

I am angry that my boss gave that promotion to this other person even though I am more qualified.

My problem: _____

_____

_____

_____

Now identify the emotion you feel (*example,* anger):_____

_____

_____

_____

Now accept the emotion by feeling it completely. *Example:* It feels really painful. I'm livid and angry. I feel

_____

_____

_____

Now that you've allowed yourself to feel the emotion, ask yourself the following questions and feel deeply for an answer:

1. Is there anything I can learn from this situation?
   Example: I can learn to stand up for myself at work and demand to be valued.

   _____

   _____

2. Is there anything amusing about this situation?
   Example: It's amusing when I imagine them both wearing Mickey Mouse ears or picture them both the size of my thumb.

   _____

   _____

3. Is there anything I can appreciate about this situation?
Example: That I know it was my vibration of lack of self-respect that attracted this situation, and I can change my vibration and attract better circumstances.

_____

_____

4. What is this emotion trying to tell me?
Example: This emotion is telling me to stand up for myself more. To raise my standards.

_____

_____

Asking yourself these kinds of questions can gradually get you feeling better about the subject, thus changing your vibration, which, in turn, creates better outer conditions.

Have you ever seen small children playing? They seem to go from rage to love to humor to tears to smiles all within an hour or so. They are allowing their guidance systems to function properly. By allowing themselves to feel, children remain more connected to their inner guidance systems and authentic selves. As adults, we must reclaim this innate ability in order to become deliberate creators of reality. Once we learn to acknowledge where we are emotionally, we can consciously feel better, shift our vibration, and attract new circumstances.

7

You Receive What You Believe

*If I have the belief that I can do it, I will surely
acquire the capacity to do it, even if I may not
have it at the beginning.*

— MAHATMA GANDHI

You may think your beliefs come from your life experience,
but in reality your life experiences come from your beliefs.
The good news is that beliefs are just habitual thoughts. They're
not so hard to change, once you change your habit of thinking/
feeling/vibrating. Remember, the best way to know if a belief
is attracting or repelling your desire is to check in with how it
makes you feel.

Remember, beliefs are easy to change with practice. But first you
have to become sensitive to how you're feeling in each moment.

To see how your habitual thoughts are affecting your attraction, write down your beliefs about a certain desire. If they
are causing you positive emotions, keep them. If you are feeling

negative, reverse them. We're going to play the opposite game, this time with our beliefs.

Finding Positively Magnetic Beliefs

We're going to attract beliefs at frequencies matching our desires, and thus draw them in. Pick three desires:

EXAMPLE

1. I'm thin and attractive.
2. I have a successful and joyous career.
3. I have a great sense of self-confidence, self-love, and self-esteem.

Your three desires

1. _____

2. _____

3. _____

Take your first desire and write down all the beliefs you have about this desire. They can be positive beliefs, but also include any negative beliefs that you associate with having this desire (*example:* "I'm not good enough to create this"). Write these down quickly. Don't think too much. Keep your pen moving for about five minutes on this exercise.

EXAMPLE

"I'm thin and attractive."

Beliefs associated with this desire: It will never happen. I've been trying to get skinny my whole life, and it never worked for long. I'm just not destined for it. I have lost weight easily in the past when I was nice to myself. Losing weight takes hard work/ discipline with diet and exercise. I'm too lazy for the work it would take to make myself look good. I starved in a past life, therefore I'm fat in this one, etc.

Your turn.

Desire #1: _____

Beliefs associated with this desire: _____

_____

_____

_____

_____

_____

Desire #2: _____

Beliefs associated with this desire: _____

_____

_____

_____

_____

_____

Desire #3: _____

Beliefs associated with this desire: _____

_____

_____

_____

You may find you have many more negative beliefs than positive ones. This is exactly why it hasn't happened yet. These resistant beliefs are vibrationally counteracting the joy of the desire, creating a tug of war between your desire and your beliefs, keeping things static. It's important to list these negative beliefs, because we now get to turn them around. First of all, let's write the positive beliefs we already listed.

EXAMPLE

Positive beliefs about getting thin. (In this example, there's only one.)

1. I have lost weight easily in the past when I was nice to myself.

This belief feels good, so we want to keep it. We want to milk it.

1. Positive beliefs about desire #1: _____

_____

_____

_____

2. Positive beliefs about desire #2: _____

_____

_____

_____

3. Positive beliefs about desire #3: _____

_____

_____

_____

If you found mostly positive beliefs, you are sending out a clear vibrational signal. Your desire is on its way. Keep feeling the joy as if the desires were already here, and soon they will be. If you don't have any positive beliefs about these things, don't be disappointed. We'll create some now.

Let's find the negative beliefs and play the opposite game—reverse them to positive beliefs.

EXAMPLE

1. *"It will never happen."*

   BECOMES

   "It will happen when I imagine it vividly."

2. *"I've been trying to get skinny my whole life and it never worked for long."*

   BECOMES

"The past doesn't equal the future. What if feeling thin first is what works this time?"

3. *"I'm just not destined for it."*
BECOMES
"I create my own destiny by what I choose to focus on."

Make sure your positive belief is semibelievable so that you can truly feel good when you read it. For instance, it might not make you feel better if you go from saying "I'm fat and ugly" to "I am the thinnest person in the world." Or "I'm always broke" may not comfortably change to "I'm richer than Bill Gates."

If these statements do make you feel good, then go for it. (It works for me to be extravagant and extreme in my opposite statements because it jolts me into believing in new possibilities.)

Reversing Negative Beliefs for Desire #1

1. _____

_____

_____

BECOMES

_____

_____

_____

2. _____

_____

_____

BECOMES

_____

_____

_____

3. _____

_____

_____

BECOMES

_____

_____

_____

Reversing Negative Beliefs for Desire #2

1. _____

_____

_____

BECOMES

_____

_____

_____

2. _____

_____

_____

BECOMES

_____

_____

_____

3. _____

_____

_____

BECOMES

_____

_____

_____

Reversing Negative Beliefs for Desire #3

1. _____

_____

_____

BECOMES

_____

_____

_____

2. _____

_____

_____

BECOMES

_____

_____

_____

3. _____

_____

_____

BECOMES

_____

_____

_____

Sense how the differing beliefs make you feel when you say them. Can you feel the joy as you say the positive statements, whereas the negative statements make you feel terrible?

Check your inner guidance on how the new replacement thoughts make you feel, realizing your guidance system is unique to you.

Turning Thoughts into Beliefs: Practice Them

This is the fun part. Write your new reversed positive beliefs on the paper with your original positive beliefs. This paper will become your new best friend. You're going to read and reread these beliefs aloud at least once a day so you can start to make them habitual.

Beliefs are only habitual thoughts. Even better than reading these thoughts aloud is to record them into a pocket tape recorder and play them over and over to yourself throughout the day. This will start to shift your vibration to the positive quickly and easily. Soon you will begin to believe these thoughts and you will feel good, thus raising your vibrations and attracting your desires.

8

Speaking Only in Positives

Be as you wish to seem.

— SOCRATES

Next, we'll address the topic of talking, since the words we utter to others and ourselves impact our feelings and affect the attracting process.

For the rest of this day and for the next thirty days, try a talking game that is fun but may also be difficult, because breaking old habits can be a challenge.

Eliminate the following words from your vocabulary:

not	*won't*
don't	*shouldn't*
can't	*haven't*
don't want	

If you find yourself using these words, stop and rephrase the statement without using them. So reverse the *don't* into a *do* before it even comes out of your mouth or shortly thereafter. This exercise is so powerful for quickly changing your beliefs that you may want to practice it for the rest of your life.

Negative words usually trigger the opposite vibration of your desires. We speak what we believe, and if we can change our beliefs whenever we speak, we're changing our vibrations. We start to send new signals to the Universe. It takes some practice, but you will find it changes your frequency almost immediately.

For example: "I don't want to go to the store today" becomes "I do want to stay home and relax today."

Think of it this way: when a child sits on Santa's lap, she doesn't whip out a Christmas list of all the things she doesn't want. That's what we do every time we focus on what we don't want. Instead, the child gives Santa her list of wants, and trusts that Santa (or the Universe) will deliver them. It's that simple. If only we could be like children at Christmas, our lives would turn around.

Because changing these words in our vocabularies helps to change our vibrations, speaking only in positives is a great habit. The Universe understands only your emotional vibrations, not your words, so changing the words helps only if it affects how you feel.

The Universe (or Law of Attraction) speaks "vibrationese." Sounds crazy, but it's true. Here's a wacky metaphorical exercise to show that you may not realize what you are sending:

Imagine that the Law of Attraction is your magic genie floating above you. S/he is from a foreign planet and understands commands only as emotions you send from your body. When you speak in words, s/he hasn't a clue what you're saying or what you desire. Anytime you feel an emotion, s/he understands it *as a command*. For example, if you say, "I want a million dollars," but you feel poor and disbelieving, your magic genie hears, "I want to be poor and disbelieving." The genie delivers anything that makes you feel poor or disbelieving. Then you say, "Why aren't my prayers ever answered?" and the genie says, "Because I don't speak your language. I understand only emotional thought vibrations. You sent me 'poor, poor, poor' and I *thought* you wanted more of that."

On the other hand, when you say, "I want a million dollars," and you are excited and grateful for all the money you have now, even if it's only a dollar, then your magic genie *understands* your emotional thought frequency of "abundance, faith, and appreciation of money." Your magic genie thinks, "Hey, that person loves and is grateful for *money*. That's what's desired, so that's what I'll deliver."

Remember, just as your dog doesn't understand when you speak about nuclear physics, the Universe doesn't understand words alone, just emotional thoughts. Start speaking clearly to your magic genie in a language s/he can understand and watch the magic begin.

So in addition to eliminating negative words from your vocabulary, try to imagine having a relationship with the Universal helpers—fairies, God, Source Energy, or however you want to imagine it, by speaking in "vibrationese." You'll be amazed at how much it improves your relationship with the Universe.

Here's a great exercise for checking in with yourself during the day to see what messages you are sending the Universe. By using this tool, you can monitor the vibrations you're sending before you get stuck in a negative signal.

Magic Genie Vibrational Check

Imagine you are floating five feet overhead, looking down on your body. You are your own magic genie, and you don't speak English, only emotional vibration. As you watch yourself "down below," what "vibes" are you getting from yourself right now? Think of the first emotions that come to mind.

EXAMPLE

As I'm floating above my body watching my emotional frequency, I seem to be sending off the signals of excitement, passion, and nervousness, wondering if my desires are going to materialize.

I am going to look at these emotions. The two I want to keep sending are excitement and passion. This means I am attracting *reasons* to be excited and passionate. As far as the emotions of "nervousness" and "wondering if my desires are going to materialize" go, I want to turn those around. I don't want more *reasons* to feel nervous about my desires.

Next, turn the emotion around and start vibrating at the opposite emotion.

- What is the opposite of "nervousness wondering if my desires are going to materialize"?
- It is "certainty and faith my desires will materialize."
- How do we get to the emotional place where we feel our desires will materialize?

First we become grateful for all the past desires that have been delivered. Below is my list of the desires I once had that are now my reality.

1. my nice sports car
2. my beautiful house
3. my two wonderful dogs
4. my parents getting healthier and healthier
5. my body being healthy

Now you try the exercise.

As I'm floating above my body watching my emotional frequency, I seem to be sending off the signals of: _____

_____

_____

_____

The positive emotions I want to keep sending out are: _____

_____

_____

_____

The negative emotions I want to turn into positive emotions are: _____

_____

_____

What are the opposite emotional signals of these negative emotions?

    1. The emotion of _____

       becomes: _____

    2. The emotion of _____

       becomes: _____

    3. The emotion of _____

       becomes: _____

How do I get myself to feel these positive emotions?

1. In what areas of my life do I already feel positive emotion #1?

_____

_____

_____

_____

(Check in with your magic genie again. Is this more on target for the emotional signal you want to send?)

2. In what areas of my life do I already feel positive emotion #2?

_____

_____

_____

_____

3. In what areas of my life do I already feel positive emotion #3?

_____

_____

_____

_____

Only through experiencing the feelings of having your desires can you access the associated beliefs. If you have the feelings of already achieving your desire, you will attract the beliefs to deliver the desire.

9

Believing Is Seeing

When you believe a thing, believe it all the way.

— WALT DISNEY

Most people think, "I'll believe it when I see it." But according to the Law of Attraction, it's "I'll believe it when I feel like I already have it." From that vibratory frequency, you attract abundant proof that your dream is possible, then more than possible, then probable, then guaranteed. All because you "feel it real."

Here's a great way to gauge whether your beliefs are aligned with your desires: *If you feel much desire, but don't have much belief that it will happen, you won't feel good when you think about what you desire.*

The failure to understand this important concept has led many to proclaim that desires are bad. (Again, we are discussing healthy desires that don't harm yourself or others.) When having a desire feels bad, it is easy to conclude that the desire itself is bad. Yet a (healthy) desire will only feel bad when you don't align it with the belief that it will happen.

It would be nice if all desires were easily achievable, no matter how we were feeling or what we believed. We would all have great wealth, perfect health, beautiful bodies, successful careers, blissful families, warm friends, fantastic vacations, spiritual growth, and even enlightenment. If these desires manifested even with our limiting beliefs, the world would be a paradise. But these desires don't come easily, because we don't believe they will, and then people suffer, thinking it was the desire that let them down rather than their limiting beliefs. This is because they are not accessing the appropriate vibrational frequencies—already living in the gratitude of the fulfilled desire. As a result, having a desire feels like a painfully lacking experience.

In the New Testament, Jesus teaches that faith heals and brings people their desired results. Their desires (to walk again, to have food for the masses, to be able to see, etc.) are manifested with faith. Jesus never said, "Don't desire to heal your body, to see again, to feed the hungry, or walk on water because desires are bad." Rather he believed it was faith that created the desired result and a lack of faith that blocked it. He believed with total faith that he could raise the dead, heal the sick, and turn water into wine.

If we could live as Jesus, as if all our desires were already fulfilled, and be grateful for the abundance in our lives now, total harmony would exist between our desires and our beliefs. Our desires would *feel* good, and they would come quickly. The Bible would have told an entirely different story if Jesus had said, "I hope he can walk again," or "I'm not sure if I can raise the dead. That's a pretty tall order."

You can bring your desire and beliefs into harmony in several ways. One method is to list all the reasons the fulfillment of your desire is possible. Imagine that you are a lawyer proving your case to a jury.

Making a Case for Your Desires

List the three desires you've been addressing throughout this book.

My three desires:

1. _____

_____

2. _____

_____

3. _____

_____

For each desire, make a case for the possibility of your having this desire. List all reasons, as if you were presenting your case to a jury.

EXAMPLE

The reasons I believe I can achieve my desire to be thin and attractive are: I've been thin in the past. If I have faith, all things are possible. When I visualized it before, it happened, etc.

Now it's your turn:

1. The reasons I believe I can achieve my desire to _____

_____

are: _____

_____

_____

_____

2. The reasons I believe I can achieve my desire to _____

_____

are: _____

_____

_____

_____

3. The reasons I believe I can achieve my desire to _____

_____

are: _____

_____

_____

_____

Another way to get your desires and beliefs aligned is to work backward, by imagining what beliefs you would have if you'd already achieved your goals.

"As if . . ." Beliefs Exercise

List the three desires you've been addressing throughout this book.

My three desires:

1. _____

2. _____

3. _____

Now list the beliefs you would have *if* you had already achieved these desires. Also, you can list the beliefs of others who already manifest your desires, such as someone who has found true love or made a lot of money.

EXAMPLE

If I had already achieved my desire to be thin and attractive, my beliefs about this desire would be:

    a. that I am one of the lucky ones when it comes to weightloss

    b. that, for me, getting thin is achievable

    c. that by eating the right foods in the right amounts, I can be thin

    d. that by exercising in the right way at the right intensity, I can get thin

1. If I had already achieved my desire to _____

_____

_____, my beliefs about this desire would be:

a. _____

_____

b. _____

_____

c. _____

_____

d. _____

_____

2. If I had already achieved my desire to _____

_____

_____, my beliefs about this desire would be:

a. _____

_____

b. _____

_____

c. _____

_____

d. _____

_____

3. If I had already achieved my desire to _____

_____

_____, my beliefs about this desire would be:

a. _____

_____

b. _____

_____

c. _____

_____

d. _____

_____

Now that we know the beliefs you would have if you had achieved your desires, list how you'd feel about having these beliefs.

EXAMPLE

1. If I already had these beliefs about my desire to be thin and attractive, it would make me feel:

a. hopeful

b. confident

c. excited

d. lucky

Your turn:

1. If I already had these beliefs about my desire to _____
   _____, it would make me
   feel:

   a. _____
      _____

   b. _____
      _____

   c. _____
      _____

   d. _____
      _____

2. If I already had these beliefs about my desire to _____
   _____, it would make me feel:

   a. _____
      _____

   b. _____
      _____

   c. _____
      _____

   d. _____
      _____

3. If I already had these beliefs about my desire to _____
   _____, it would make me feel:

a. _____

_____

b. _____

_____

c. _____

_____

d. _____

_____

This is such a powerful exercise. In just those few minutes that you spent answering these questions, you harmonized your beliefs with your desires.

Now the Law of Attraction will go to work and attract even more reasons for you to believe in your desires. This will create more good feelings, and in turn create more beliefs. Before you know it, your desires are delivered to you.

This previous exercise also uncovers your beliefs about these desires, and you may uncover beliefs you didn't know you had. If you find beliefs that aren't empowering, then you get to play the opposite game to help you create opposite beliefs.

Remember, beliefs are changeable. It's possible, with practice, to create a whole new set of empowering beliefs. Also, beliefs are just habitual thoughts, so as we learn to change our thoughts and feelings, we will naturally change our beliefs.

It is helpful to identify beliefs you share with others. Sometimes we are unconscious about our own limiting beliefs, but we can easily detect them in others. When you hear someone expressing a limiting belief, go ahead and ask yourself, "Do I have this same limiting belief?" When they speak a belief that doesn't feel good to you, such as "A good man is hard to find," or "Money doesn't grow on trees," or "Everything I eat goes to my waist," you can notice if you share that belief or not.

If someone around you verbalizes disharmonious beliefs, you can play the opposite game in your imagination. It's fun to play this game in your mind, and it helps keep you amused and positive around negative people. For example, if you hear someone say, "The world is going to hell in a handbasket," you can think the opposite belief, such as "There is so much well-being in this world. The sun comes up every day and people do kind things for others all the time."

Remember, only you get to decide how to focus your frequencies. It is always ultimately up to you to think empowering thoughts and feel empowering feelings.

Focus is an important aspect of controlling your beliefs. You can focus on the beliefs that make you feel good and empowered or you can focus on the beliefs that make you feel bad. We always have the option to choose between positive or negative beliefs. This choice is a beautiful gift, since it enables us to control our personal realities.

10

The Vibrational Power of Love and Appreciation

God has poured out his love into our hearts.

— ROMANS 5:5

It's been said, "Love is the answer." But what is the question? Why, throughout human history, has love been touted as the be-all and end-all? Romantic love, brotherly love, maternal love, platonic love, forbidden love, love of art or a hobby or a sport, instinctual love, spiritual love, chivalrous love, love of God, natural love—love, love, love.

LOVE.

What is it about those four letters and the vibrations they summon?

For starters, love is the highest frequency from which we can vibrate. It the closest we can become to Pure Spirit. Love is *who* and *what* we are. When we choose to love, we are more Ourselves, with a capital *O*. When we choose not to love, we are like actors in a play, pretending to be other characters.

Love and similar vibrations of appreciation, compassion, tenderness, kindness, generosity, and nurturance raise our frequencies to blissful levels because those vibrations are the most natural to us as Spiritual Beings.

Here is a game to determine how quickly love and appreciation can lift our frequencies. Play this with me to switch your focus in the blink of an eye from feeling lousy to feeling grand.

Right now, think of three things in your life that aren't going well and list them.

EXAMPLE

Three Things That Aren't Going Well in My Life
1. My career as a singer
2. I am lonely and want a mate
3. I need money

Your turn:

Three Things That Aren't Going Well in My Life
1. _____

_____

2. _____

_____

3. _____

_____

Notice how this makes you feel. Pretty lousy, right? Your frequencies are feeling pretty low right now, aren't they? Do you feel like you could feel down for the rest of the day?

Now try this. List three things that are going wonderfully in your life—things you LOVE and APPRECIATE.

EXAMPLE

Three Things That I Love and Appreciate in My Life
   1. My children love me unconditionally.
   2. I live in a great house.
   3. My parents are really kind to me.

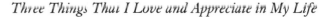

Three Things That I Love and Appreciate in My Life

   1. _____

   _____

   2. _____

   _____

   3. _____

Did you notice a change in the way you feel? Miraculous, isn't it? Now let's do it even more quickly, to show how love changes your frequency.

List one thing about your life you don't like:

I don't like _____

_____

_____

Now list one thing about your life you love:

I love _____

_____

_____

Now do it even faster. Another thing about my life I don't like is:

I don't like _____

_____

_____

Another thing about my life I love:

I love _____

_____

_____

Do it again. Another thing I don't like about my life is:

I don't like _____

_____

_____

Another thing about my life I love:

I love _____

_____

_____

Can you see how quickly the vibration of love changes the way you feel? Did you feel the difference emotionally? How about physically? Changing your focus to love caused your vibration to raise and you to feel better.

In every moment of every day, you can feel better and attract more love to you if you decide to focus on love. There are infinite opportunities to turn your attention toward love and appreciation. It's your choice. So much is wonderful in this world and in your life.

Several years ago, I visited a friend, a mother with a three-month-old child. Everything was joyful, and everyone was emanating well-being. I had a huge grin on my face when I left. The baby was vibrating at "love" so strongly that he uplifted everyone around him. When I arrived home, my father was watching the news, which focused on a possible terrorist attack in the United States. I suddenly went from feeling a perfect sense of peace to uneasiness. Choosing to use my Law of Attraction skills, I remembered the baby's face and laughter. Suddenly, by tuning my signal to the vibration of love and appreciation, I felt the love again. I turned away from the newscast and walked outside to smell some flowers. I focused on their beautiful fragrance and color. I remained in love.

It is empowering to know you are in the driver's seat of your life. You can decide to focus on love or fear, the flowers or the weeds, the dog or the dog poop. It's all up to you.

Remember, changing your vibration to love is just as easy as changing your focus.

11

Get High by Giving Love

Think about it, there must be a higher love
Down in the heart or hidden in the stars above

—STEVE WINWOOD

When I feel stuck on something negative, I increase my vibrations by giving love. Giving love unclogs the vibrational drain so that it returns to a high-frequency level. It speeds things up and quickly lifts my spirits.

Consider these facts about giving love:

1. It makes you feel good.
2. It's a free and legal way to get high.
3. Giving unconditional love, with no strings, for the sheer joy of it, *always attracts by law* even *more* love back to you. It may not be given from the person who you gave it to, but it *will* come from somewhere.
4. Focusing on a person's positive attributes is an incredible way to give love.

5. Love isn't so much about what you do for someone. It's how you feel about someone.

6. Over the years, I have noticed that the clients who give love to many people, even those they don't know, are the happiest. What does that tell you?

7. When I feel hurt or angry with someone, it never feels good to get back at him or her. It feels a lot better to send them love by focusing on their positive attributes. Revenge feels like concrete in my gut, whereas love feels feathery and light.

When I get stuck focused on a negative, I feel better if I:

1. Do something kind for a stranger.

2. List all the good attributes of the people or situation in question.

3. Take time to appreciate the people/animals who adore me.

4. Realize that by spreading love, my life becomes abundant in every way.

Learning to create positive beliefs about love into my outlook on life helps me become more loving. Some of the most empowering beliefs involve the concept of love, and these beliefs are pivotal in helping me consistently raise my frequencies.

Empowering beliefs I hold about love:

1. Love is the highest frequency there is.

2. The more love I give, the more love I receive.

3. The only real abundance in the world is love.

4. If I am vibrating at a frequency of love, my material needs will easily be met.

5. Love opens doors.

6. God is Love.

7. Love is the invisible force that runs the Universe.

8. If I want to feel loved, I have to love myself.

9. If I want to feel loved, I have to love others.

10. Appreciation and love are similar frequencies.

11. It's easy for me to love when I focus on a person's positive qualities.

Best belief of all: *There are infinite things to love about everyone because everyone is infinite.*

I repeat this belief when I have a difficult time feeling love. It always makes me feel better. Sometimes I insert individual names: there are infinite things to love about Charlie because Charlie is infinite.

What beliefs do you want to have about love? Beliefs are the blueprints for creating your life. Change your beliefs, and you will change your focus. Changing your focus changes your vibrations. Changing your vibrations changes what you attract, which transforms your life.

When we vibrate at "love," by the Law of Attraction, we attract like frequencies. That's why people who give the most love to themselves and others are the most loved. They attract the frequencies at which they send.

Some people have a hard time receiving love because they are not aligned with love. They focus on the lack of love. The good news is that we can still love them. We decide how we vibrate.

We can look with compassion on the person having difficulty being loved, realizing s/he, too, is a Spiritual Being. S/he is Love. S/he, too, at the core, is pure positive energy. We can relate from this broader perspective. Thus, we keep our frequencies high, undeterred by others, and we attract more love as we stay at those higher vibrations.

One of my favorite stories is this one about the Buddha.

Hearing that Buddha was enlightened, a man traveled far to see him. But this man was full of hatred. When he found the Buddha, he swore at him, cursed him, and called him names day and night. The Buddha continued to meditate quietly with a warm smile on his face. After several days, the man grew tired, as he hadn't broken down the Buddha at all.

Finally, one morning the Buddha called the man to him. The Buddha said, "Let me ask you a question. If a man brings me a gift and I refuse to accept it, to whom does the gift belong?"

The man thought for a minute and said, "To the one who gave it."

The Buddha smiled and nodded. Then he said, "Then if you come to me with the gift of hatred and I refuse to accept it, to whom does the hatred belong?" The man gasped, "To me."

After that, the man became a follower of the Buddha and was happy for the lesson he learned about love.

In this story, the Buddha decided to hold his note of love and remain at that vibration, no matter what the man's vibrational level.

We choose our own vibrations, including the vibration of love when someone else has temporarily lost his/her way.

When Jesus said, "Forgive them, Father, they know not what they do," he was expressing that they didn't remember that they, too, were one with the Source, one with Love, one with God. Had they remembered, they wouldn't have acted from these disconnected states. People who seem disconnected, negative, or even hateful have temporarily forgotten who they are and have strayed from the frequency of Love.

12

Turn Up Your Frequency by Plugging into Your Source

Our Creator would never had made such lovely
days, and given us the deep hearts to enjoy them,
above and beyond all thought, unless we were
meant to be immortal.

—NATHANIEL HAWTHORNE

What is God? Who is God? What is the Invisible Force beyond the visible world? These questions are as old as time. Though the answers are beyond the scope of this book, we will explore what "God" means to you in regards to the Law of Attraction.

As we discussed in the beginning of the book, scientists have confirmed that all matter is made up of energy, including us. We are all essentially energy that is vibrating at certain frequencies. What scientists are now discovering is that our thoughts and emotions are vibrating on different frequencies, depending on the vibratory makeup of these thoughts/emotions. When we think thoughts of love, we feel more fluid, more connected. When we think thoughts of hate or fear, we feel heavy, separate from our surroundings.

I believe that we are Spiritual Beings dwelling in bodies, and that we as Spiritual Beings are vibrating at extremely higher frequencies than the denser energies of our bodies.

When we are thinking thoughts of joy, happiness, abundance, and love, we are more in alignment with our Spiritual Self, which vibrates at a very high frequency. This matching of energies between our thoughts and feelings with our Spiritual Self creates a sense of connectedness and oneness. This connection is really with Ourselves, our higher vibrating Spiritual Self. When we feel negative emotions, they are uncomfortable because they are vibrating at a much slower rate than our Spiritual Selves, therefore creating a sense of dissonance and disconnection. When we are vibrating at these lower frequencies, it is as if we have cut ourselves off from our own Spirit.

We can lift vibrations quickly by talking directly to our Spiritual Nature, who is constantly vibrating on high, happy frequencies. We can communicate with our Spiritual Selves through prayer, meditation, speaking with or writing as our Spiritual Self.

Connecting with that energy is like plugging in your appliance and animating it with energy. It's your job to plug yourself in. How?

People can choose to connect with Christ, Buddha, their Inner Voice, the Great Spirit, Nature Intelligence, Devas, God, Goddess, Angels, Spirit Guides, the Fairy Realm, or whatever appeals to their individual preferences. All of these beings are a part of your Spiritual Self and are vibrating at that same high frequency where all is always well.

Each of our Spirit Selves is a part of the Source of Oneness, which is the One Intelligence that involves and evolves everyone and everything. This Oneness is, in reality, unnameable because it operates at a frequency beyond language. It's challenging to think of words to describe it.

You may feel a strong connection with Krishna or Allah or your Higher Power or Pure Energy. There are so many names for "Source." *It doesn't matter what you call your Source. It only matters that you call on your Source.*

Beings who are "plugged in" have the following traits:

1. They vibrate higher and faster than most because they have no resistance to love.
2. Their answers are based on love and inclusion.
3. They see the world with a "big picture" perspective.
4. They seem extremely joyful.
5. They are teachers by example.
6. They help those seeking to get "plugged in."
7. They easily create their desires, often beyond the physical laws of the Universe.

My intention is to help you become more plugged in until you realize that you, too, are one with this Source.

Our greatest desire in life is to realize that we are already one with this Power, with this Force of creative, infinite Love.

Intend to connect with your Spirit Self now. Talk to him, her, it, them. Feel your energy. Ask about raising your frequencies and becoming more plugged in, more deliberate in creating the life you want.

Write your observations and feelings below. You might want to write a conversation between you and your Spirit Self asking him/her/it any questions you have. Then answer from his/her/its perspective.

Develop the lifelong habit of talking to your Spiritual Self and asking questions. Ask to get connected to him/her/it. My Spiritual Self talks to me when I am meditating after having quieted my mind. She appears to me as a glowing female presence and is always full of great guidance and unconditional love.

One thing is for sure. You will receive help from your Spirit Self if you ask for it. This guidance is always available to you. Experiment with what form of communication feels right to you, and then ask for insight about keeping your vibrations joyful and loving. It's what life is all about.

Remember, you, too, are an angel, a Spiritual Being, and a part of that spark of All-knowingness. Connecting with your higher vibrating Spiritual Nature will give your life more meaning, flow, guidance, and purpose. What's more, it will make it easier for you to manifest the things you want. If you consistently vibrate at the high frequencies of your Spiritual Self, you will be delighted by what the Law of Attraction helps you attract back into your life.

Section Two

❖

A Book of Games
to Attract Your Desires

This section contains more games to help you raise your frequencies and attract your desires. These games are powerful, but they must be played with sheer joy to be fully effective. Play them until your desires are fulfilled. Then play them again when you have new desires. This section can help you realize your desires, big and little, for the rest of your life. The games can become your trusted, lifelong dream-making tools.

It's often beneficial to play these games with at least one other person. You could start a *Feel It Real!* focus group and practice the games with one another. Follow your inner guidance to determine if you feel more joy working with others or alone.

Certain props enhance the experience. Below are some helpful items to have around when you play these games.

- a tape recorder (a mini/portable would be ideal)
- a "magic wand" (Be creative: It could be a stick with an aluminum foil star on the end, a soap bubble wand, a store-bought magic wand for children, etc.)
- a mirror
- a journal
- poster board

- scissors
- glue stick or tape
- old magazines and catalogs

As you practice these games, it's important to work at your own pace, and to use an approach that works for you. You have to follow what feels good to you in each moment. Some days, Game 15 might feel good to you: another day, Game 10. It doesn't matter that your preferences change, because change is natural.

You may need to play a certain game for many days or even weeks to get the hang of it. If you find yourself taking a game too seriously, stop immediately and go do something fun. Remember to let your emotions guide you toward what feels good.

Games to Create a Life You Love

Game 1

HOLD THAT NOTE

❖

Love, love, love, that is the soul of genius.

—Wolfgang Amadeus Mozart

This is a fun exercise for those of you who are musically inclined—even if the inclination is just toward enjoying music. Music is vibrational. If you strike a tuning fork, a similar tuning fork will resonate. But tuning forks that are tuned to notes different from those around them will not cause those others to resonate. So it is with thought.

Imagine for a second that you are a giant tuning fork. Pick the note you want to be tuned to. Your note could be ecstasy or love or fame or mystery or gratitude or abundance or love— whatever you most desire to attract. If you want true love, tune your fork to "lovable." If you want dollars, tune to "wealth."

Now close your eyes. Imagine that someone has hit a note with a xylophone mallet, and you, the tuning fork, begin to resonate the emotional "note" you've chosen.

Try to "hold the note" to a count of at least sixteen seconds. Holding the note for this long sets your vibration at the desired frequency. Imagine that your whole body, even the electromagnetic field around your body, is vibrating at this "note" for sixteen seconds.

Sometimes when I do this exercise, I can feel the vibration buzzing through my body. This is simple and fun, yet it's a powerful exercise. Try to hold the note every day for thirty days and you will reset your dominant vibration to this desire.

Once you can easily vibrate at the emotion of your choice, move on to a different "note" and begin to resonate there.

Game 2

FIND THE FEELING PLACE

⋅⋅⋄⋅⋅

*Though we travel the world over to find
the beautiful, we must carry it with us
or we find it not.*

— RALPH WALDO EMERSON

Are you familiar with the feeling you would have if your desire were already fulfilled? Once you feel emotional familiarity with the vibration of already having your desires, you attract them to you.

Think of a desire that you have. First, write the emotions you feel about the desire, both positive and negative. For example: I want to get my project financed.

My Emotions Now:

confused, desire, stuck, blocked, victimized, longing, doubt, hope, hurt, jealousy, discouragement, futility, sadness, hopelessness, powerless, unlucky, depression, anger

The Emotions I Will Have:

> *excitement, fun, lighthearted, levity, loved, appreciation, flowing love, gratitude, blessedness, relief, lucky, ease, empowered, appreciated, connected, "at one," creative, humbled, loving, savoring, reveling, deliciousness, helpful, uplifted, close to God*

Your turn. Desire: _____

_____

My Emotions Now:

_____

_____

_____

_____

The Emotions I Will Have:

_____

_____

_____

_____

Take an honest look at your responses and ask yourself, "Is it any surprise that my desire hasn't yet been fulfilled?"

Make a twenty-four-hour commitment to prioritize getting into these feelings. If your current emotions are predominantly negative, stop all action toward this desire right now and commit first to feeling the emotions you will have when you think about your desire. Do this by visualizing, appreciating, laughing, having fun, or using any of the other games in this book.

Game 3

IT ALREADY HAPPENED

❖

*It's a funny thing about life; if you refuse to accept
anything but the best, you very often get it.*

— W. Somerset Maugham

Think of one of your biggest desires.
Write it here: _____

_____

_____

Now imagine how you would feel if you already had that
desire. What does it feel like when you first get it? Describe
your emotions. _____

_____

_____

_____

_____

_____

What does it feel like six months after you've received it?
Describe your emotions. _____

_____

_____

_____

_____

_____

_____

What does it feel like a year after you've received it? Describe your emotions. _____

_____

_____

_____

_____

_____

_____

What does it feel like five years after you've received it? Describe your emotions. _____

_____

_____

_____

_____

_____

_____

What does it feel like twenty years after you've received it?
Describe your emotions. _____

_____

_____

_____

_____

_____

As you begin to become more familiar with the vibration of already having your desire, you will be sending out a vibration that matches its frequency, thus attracting it to you. Now list the ten most dominant emotions or vibrations you would have if you already had this desire.

1. _____
2. _____
3. _____
4. _____
5. _____
6. _____
7. _____
8. _____
9. _____
10. _____

From my experience, I have found that gratitude is one of the most commonly felt emotions for anyone who has his/her desire fulfilled. So take a minute and be thankful for this desire before it gets here. This is guaranteed to make you feel good, and if you feel good about your desire, you will attract it.

Game 4

MATCH THE FREQUENCY

⋯⋄⋯

If you can dream it, you can do it.

— WALT DISNEY

This is a fun game for anyone who wants to positively use their imaginations. We all have imaginations. Some people use theirs to worry about the future and imagine "worst case" scenarios, but your imagination can also be used to help you get into the feeling place of already having your desires. Write one of your desires here.

Example: I desire to be a millionaire by doing only the things that I love.

Your desire: _____

_____

_____

Think of someone who already possesses the thing you desire. It could be someone you know, personally or not. For

example, a billionaire who does only things he loves would be
Paul McCartney. By pursuing his love of music, he became a
billionaire.

Close your eyes and relax. Take a deep breath. Imagine that you
are the person you've chosen. Breathe as you think s/he breathes.
What does this person believe about the thing you desire? Did it
feel hard for them to get it? Probably not, because they already
have it. Now imagine what vibrational signal s/he emits daily
about this thing you desire. What are this person's beliefs about
this thing you desire? Does s/he think s/he deserves it?

If I were using Paul McCartney as my example, I would
believe that it was easy for me to get paid for having fun while
playing music. Regarding money and work, I'd imagine that
Paul McCartney vibrates at fun, joy, childishness, bliss, creativity, ease, blessedness, wealth, and appreciation. Now that
you've found the frequency that you imagine this person
might hold, imagine for about a minute vibrating at the same
frequency.

Imagine you are a radio emitting "101. funjoychildishness-
blisscreativityeaseblessednesswealthappreciation" or whatever
vibration you think this person holds. When you are finished holding that frequency for one solid minute, record your thoughts
here.

_____

_____

_____

_____

_____

_____

_____

This is a powerful exercise for retraining your vibration toward already having your desires.

Game 5

WHAT BELIEFS WOULD YOU HAVE?

∴

If you can believe, all things are possible
to him who believeth.

— MARK 9:23

Think of a desire and imagine the beliefs you would have if you already possessed the desire. For example, imagine that your desire is to find true love. You wave a magic wand, and the partner of your dreams has appeared. What beliefs would you now have about this aspect of your life?

They could be "I am so lovable" or "I believe in 'happily ever after'" or "I deserve to be adored by a man/woman." Write your desire here:

Desire: _____

_____

_____

_____

Write ten beliefs you would have if you already had your desire. State them in the present tense.

1. _____
   _____

2. _____
   _____

3. _____
   _____

4. _____
   _____

5. _____
   _____

6. _____
   _____

7. _____
   _____

8. _____
   _____

9. _____
   _____

10. _____
    _____

Read these beliefs aloud into your tape recorder. Listen to them once a day for thirty days.

Game 6

THE COLLAGE

∴

Instead of fighting your problems,
picture your way out of them.

— VERNON HOWARD

Cut out specific images of your desires from magazines—for example, someone vacationing in the Caribbean, your dream car, a pair of Jimmy Choo shoes, someone practicing your ideal career, two people in love. This is a fun exercise, because it involves having constant visuals of what your desires look like. Now tape or glue these pictures on a poster board for you to look at each day. Look at these images each morning, and imagine what it would feel like to already be living out these visions.

This exercise really helps you vibrate at "you already have it," the frequency that attracts our desires.

Game 7

CLOSE YOUR EYES

Just because a man lacks the use of his eyes
doesn't mean he lacks vision.

—STEVIE WONDER

Too often we let the outer conditions of our lives determine how we feel and thus what we attract. That's fine if what we are looking at is something we like. But if what we see around us is something we do not like, then by observing it and focusing on it we keep attracting more of it into our lives.

This game is very simple; it's designed to help you to stop focusing on what you don't want and to imagine what you do want. To play, just close your eyes and imagine that you are in the exact surroundings you would be in if your desire had already manifested itself.

For example, if you are currently living in a tiny apartment but you would like to be living in a brand-new home, close your eyes and imagine that you are currently sitting in that home. With your eyes closed, in your mind's eye, where in the room are you? How tall are the ceilings? What is the floor made of? What color are the walls? If you want to win an Academy Award, imagine that you are at the award ceremony. Who is sitting in front of you? Who is sitting behind and beside you? Who is standing at the podium? How high are the ceilings? What colors are the curtains and walls? Now as you imagine this vividly, see if you can evoke the emotions from currently being in these surroundings. Describe how it makes you feel.

_____

_____

_____

_____

_____

_____

_____

_____

_____

Closing your eyes can open your eyes to creating your dreams!

Game 8

DRAW YOUR DESIRE

⋅⋄⋅

Every artist dips his brush into his own soul, and
paints his own nature into his pictures.

—Henry Ward Beecher

This is a fun game, whether or not you consider yourself artistic. This game allows you to do two things: first, to be lighthearted about your desires, and second, to make your desire seem more real by making it real on paper. Doing this extracts our desires from inside our mind and brings it into the two-dimensional art world.

In the following space, or on a separate piece of paper, take some pens, pencils, or crayons and draw an image of your desire fulfilled. Use color to enhance the vision. The drawings can be symbolic or literal, depending on what makes you feel good.

For example, if you desire to be more joyful, draw an image of what you being joyful might look like. It could be a brightly colored drawing of you smiling in the sunshine or maybe an abstract drawing of what joy feels like to you. If you have a certain career goal, draw a picture of yourself literally or symbolically having that career success.

If you want to manifest self-love, you might draw a symbolic picture of yourself as self-loving. For example, it could be a drawing of you giving yourself a hug with the words "I love you" written at the bottom. If you use a separate piece of paper, you can post the drawing where you'll see it each day. Do this with many diffcrent desires and have fun with it.

Game 9

THE TV GAME

❖

*One supreme fact which I have discovered is that it
is not willpower, but fantasy-imagination
that creates. Imagination is the creative force.
Imagination creates reality.*

— RICHARD WAGNER

If you are somebody who has a hard time visualizing yourself having your desires, this game may be helpful. It's a new way to watch TV that involves seeking out images of people who are already living your dream.

Learn to watch TV as if you were flipping through a catalog, seeking out images that help you get into the feeling place of having your desire.

This is different from watching TV in the traditional sense, because it's not about getting lost in the story lines or letting the shows dictate your mood. It's more about you seeking the images that help you feel it real, just as you did in the collage exercise.

Here's how it works. Say you have always wanted to vacation in Hawaii. With all the reality and educational television that is on these days, it's very likely that you could flip to a station where someone is vacationing in Hawaii. If you have a hard time visualizing yourself vacationing there, just imagine how this person on TV feels. Seeing them walking on the beach and enjoying the sunset can more easily get you into the feeling place. Before you turn on the TV, decide what you would like to create or manifest. It might help you focus if you write it down. Now turn on the TV and flip through the channels until you find images of somebody who is living this desire or something similar to it. Imagine how it would feel to be experiencing the same circumstances that they are experiencing. Really go for the emotions of having this desire until you feel like you have the desire right now. When you are done, you can recall that TV show or that situation on TV to help you remember the feeling place of having that desire. In this way, even watching TV can become an empowering creative workshop.

Game 10

THREE-MINUTE VISUALIZATION

⋄⋄⋄

It is the mind that makes the body rich.

— WILLIAM SHAKESPEARE

Sit in a comfortable place and close your door to the outer world so that you can focus within. Think of one of your desires and visualize having it with all of your senses. What is the weather like in your vision? Is it hot or cold? Where are you sitting or standing? If you are sitting, what does the seat feel like underneath you? If you are standing, what surface are you standing on? Hardwood? Grass? Carpet? Who is there with you?

Now imagine yourself happy in your visualization, smiling, even laughing, so the "having" of your vision brings you joy. Now, notice any other details in this vision. What clothes are you wearing? How do they feel on your body? What are the smells around you? What are the sounds around you? Vividly imagine this with all of your senses. When your three minutes of intense visualizing are finished, say out loud, "And it was good," to complete the visualization process.

Do this same visualization for three minutes every day, and watch what synchronicities unfold as your desire is magnetized toward you.

Games to Create
Abundance and Wealth

Game 11

MULTIMILLIONAIRE'S SPENDING GAME

⬥

*The day, water, sun, moon, night—I do not have
to purchase these things with money.*

— PLAUTUS

This game will force you to dream bigger than you've ever imagined. With the number of dollars you'll be "spending," you'll be vibrating at the frequencies of the megawealthy. It's one thing to imagine buying a new car, and another to imagine buying the original ruby red slippers from the *Wizard of Oz* (millions of dollars), or a $29 million estate on the beach at La Jolla, California. This exercise expands our imagination muscle to the point where we vibrate at ABUNDANCE whenever we play.

In this version of the prosperity game, we need a checkbook register, an artist's drawing pad, a glue stick, and magazines or access to the Internet. Some great magazines for this exercise feature dream real estate, expensive jewelry, and travel desti-nations. Online, you'll find many places to purchase expensive items, such as Christie's and Sotheby's.

On day one you begin by "depositing" $1 million, and you are then required to "spend" that million by browsing through catalogs, magazines, or shop windows, or online. On day two, you get $2 million, and are expected to spend all $2 million during that day. Play each day, adding $1 million until you reach $20 million, then start over. Enjoy the wealth.

Day One:	*$1 million*
Day Two:	*$2 million*
Day Three:	*$3 million*

. . . and so on until you hit $20 million on day 20. Then start over again.

Paste photographs or descriptions of the items you've "bought" into your artist's pad. Review items from previous days to get ideas for the next day's "purchases."

For example, if one day you buy a sprawling estate for three million dollars, the next day you might want to buy furniture or art for your mansion.

You'll notice that amazing things begin to happen. Your vi-bration level radiates at, "I have way more money than I can spend each day." So make sure you spend the money each day if possible, or you may find yourself having to spend one hundred million dollars in one day. You know it's working when you start to feel a little tired from all the spending. When you ask yourself, "Haven't I spent it all yet?" you are reprogramming your vibration toward an overflow of ABUNDANCE.

As your frequency begins to vibrate at this level of abundance, you will become a money magnet and attract big chunks of cash.

How do you feel about money before playing the game?

_____

_____

_____

_____

After having played for a few weeks, how do you feel about money? Notice any changes you've made in your vibration level?

_____

_____

_____

_____

Game 12

WANT WHAT YOU HAVE

⋅⁘⋅

Never lose an opportunity to see anything that
is beautiful. It is God's handwriting—a wayside
sacrament. Welcome it in every fair face,
every fair sky, every fair flower.

—RALPH WALDO EMERSON

This exercise will give you examples of all the desires you once had that have now been fulfilled. Think of ten things that you now have in your life, but that at one time were only desires. Fortunately you allowed these desires to come to you. Let's appreciate that feeling.

List ten things, big or small, that at one time were just desires but are now a part of your life.

My Examples	*Your "I Have It Now" List*
1. Starbucks latte	1. _____
2. Jaguar (car)	2. _____
3. House	3. _____

4. Dogs	4. _____
5. Spiritual book	5. _____
6. Husband	6. _____
7. Furniture	7. _____
8. Wedding	8. _____
9. Chinese food	9. _____
10. Big-screen TV	10. _____

Next, write down five things you appreciate about having each "I Have It Now" desire. As you do this, take note of your vibration. It's at the perfect mix of desire and receiving. Practice this regularly, and as you do, your vibration will become more familiar and comfortable with the feeling of allowing in desire.

My "I Have It Now"
   1. My Starbucks latte.

"Appreciations"
   1. The taste.
   2. The feeling of the warm milk.
   3. The enjoyable drive, listening to beautiful music while on my way to one of the many Starbucks.
   4. The helpful lady who sold it to me.
   5. Getting to spend time with my husband.

Now it's your turn.

"*I Have It Now*"   "*Appreciations*"

1. _____   1._____

2. _____   2._____

3. _____   3._____

4. _____   4._____

5. _____   5._____

As you begin to appreciate your desires that already have been fulfilled, you'll notice yourself becoming more familiar with the vibration of allowing in desire.

Game 13

THANK YOU, UNIVERSE

·:·

He who is not contented with what he has,
would not be contented with what he
would like to have.

— Socrates

This is one of my favorite games because it combines the vibrations of GRATITUDE, ALLOWANCE, and DESIRE by almost tricking your vibration into letting yourself have things you previously weren't allowing. We start by getting you to vibrate at gratitude for what you've already allowed into your life.

Thank the Universe out loud for ten things you now have but that once were just desires. For example: "Thank you, Universe, for that beautiful car I wanted"; "Thank you, Universe, for the new house I wanted." Now write yours here:

Thank you, Universe, for _____

Thank you, Universe, for _____

Thank you, Universe, for _____

Thank you, Universe, for _____

Thank you, Universe, for _____

Thank you, Universe, for _____

Thank you, Universe, for _____

Thank you, Universe, for _____

Thank you, Universe, for _____

Thank you, Universe, for _____

Write ten things you don't have, as if you were already given them. Then thank the Universe with the same emotion that you just used for the things you do have. For example, you may not have the love of your life at this moment, so you would say, "Thank you, Universe, for giving me the love of my life."

Thank you, Universe, for _____

Thank you, Universe, for _____

Thank you, Universe, for _____

Thank you, Universe, for _____

Thank you, Universe, for _____

Thank you, Universe, for _____

Thank you, Universe, for _____

Thank you, Universe, for _____

Thank you, Universe, for _____

Thank you, Universe, for _____

This exercise will familiarize you with the feelings or vibrations of gratitude and allow these desires to enter into your life.

Now read them out loud, alternating one from the first list with one from the second list. This will trick your vibration into feeling grateful for your unfulfilled desires.

Game 14

ALREADY WEALTHY

❖

When I bought my farm, I did not know what a
bargain I had in bluebirds, daffodils and thrushes;
as little did I know what sublime mornings
and sunsets I was buying.

—RALPH WALDO EMERSON

How can we train ourselves to be as wealthy as Bill Gates or Donald Trump? By training our minds to live in gratitude.

For the next thirty days, let's vibrate at "wealth" in a simple way. Buy a green journal, or put something green on the cover of the journal. (This color will help us to feel abundant.) Every day, list twenty ways that you already feel wealthy. Write on the title page: "The Ways That I'm Already Wealthy."

Each day, write down twenty things in your book. Make it a habit, like brushing your teeth. In fact, believe it or not, this may be a more important habit than brushing your teeth.

Here are some examples:

Today, when my dog curled up with me, I felt wealthy.
The weather today was gorgeous, and it made me feel wealthy.
My child's smile makes me feel wealthy.

You may not think that feeling wealthy in ways other than finances can bring you financial abundance. Many people, including myself, are testaments to the fact that feeling wealthy and grateful will attract more wealth of all forms—including financial.

Appreciating the wealth we already have teaches us to more readily appreciate new financial wealth when it arrives. Remember to appreciate all the dollars that are now in your bank account, or *have ever been* in your bank account. If you receive dollars and you don't appreciate them, how do you expect to attract more?

Financial wealth does not *create* abundance consciousness. It is the *result* of abundance consciousness. So get wealthy first; then watch the dollars come.

Game 15

"SINCE MONEY IS NO OBJECT"

❖

*Without leaps of imagination, or dreaming, we
lose the excitement of possibilities. Dreaming, after
all, is a form of planning.*

—GLORIA STEINEM

So often we limit our desires because of our beliefs that we'll
never have enough money to finance them. We think that
we have to first figure out how to make a lot of money, and then
we can let ourselves dream big. The truth about the Law of Attraction is that it's more important for us to dream big first and
then let the "hows" take care of themselves. The Universe has
infinite means to bring your dreams to you if you will only allow
yourself to live from the feeling of the dream already fulfilled.

For now let's take money out of the equation in order to
truly dream big.

List ten things you would want to do/be/have if money were
no object, meaning you already have so much money, it doesn't
even enter into the equation (say you have a billion dollars).

For example:

Since money is no object, I want to own my own racehorse.
Since money is no object, I want to tour the world via cruise ship.
Since money is no object, I want to quit my job and start painting landscapes.

Your turn:

1. Since money is no object, I want to _____

   _____

2. Since money is no object, I want to _____

   _____

3. Since money is no object, I want to _____

   _____

4. Since money is no object, I want to _____

   _____

5. Since money is no object, I want to _____

   _____

6. Since money is no object, I want to _____

   _____

7. Since money is no object, I want to _____

   _____

8. Since money is no object, I want to _____

   _____

9. Since money is no object, I want to _____

_____

10. Since money is no object, I want to _____

_____

Remember to keep dreaming big and to remind yourself that "money is no object."

Game 16

TWENTY BELIEFS ABOUT
YOUR IDEAL BODY

❖

Whether you think you can or
think you can't, you're right.

—HENRY FORD

If all it takes to manifest your ideal body is to desire it, to believe it is already yours and to expect it, then why isn't it here yet? Any delay in the delivery of having the body of your dreams is usually caused by not having enough faith that it will come. This exercise helps you align your beliefs with your desires.

For this game, list the specific desire you have for your body. It could be a desire for more health, more energy, or a new figure. For example, you may desire a thinner body. You may be quite clear on the kind of body you want. You may even appreciate all the details of it. But now let's get into the "believing" place where you can actually have that ideal body. List twenty reasons why it is possible or probable that you will have that desire. For example:

Desire: a thinner body
Reasons:

1. I've been thin in the past.
2. When I exercise a lot, I get thin.
3. If I can visualize it, it's possible.
4. I'm determined.
5. I'm committed.
6. My wife/husband is supportive.
7. There are infinite exercise regimens and eating plans out there; one is bound to work for me.
8. I'm going to take my time and do it right.
9. My body responds to the mental pictures my mind gives it; if I give it thin images, it will respond.

Desire: _____

_____

Reasons:

1. _____
2. _____
3. _____

4. _____

5. _____

6. _____

7. _____

8. _____

9. _____

10. _____

11. _____

12. _____

13. _____

14. _____

15. _____

16. _____

17. _____

18. _____

19. _____

20. _____

Read these aloud to yourself each day, along with visualizing yourself already living in your ideal body, and watch the Universe work its magic.

Game 17

LIVE IN YOUR PERFECT BODY NOW

-:::-

I am enough of an artist to draw freely upon
my imagination. Imagination is more important
than knowledge. Knowledge is limited.
Imagination encircles the world.

— ALBERT EINSTEIN

If you had your perfect body now, what would it feel like? Write down a description of living a whole day in your ideal body. Describe it in detail. What does it feel like to move about in that body? What is your energy level? How do you look? What do you do for activities? What emotions do you feel?

_____

_____

_____

_____

_____

_____

_____

_____

_____

_____

Afterward, have a conversation with your ideal future body. Ask it what you need to know to live in those feelings now. Ask your ideal future body how it feels being in that body. What thoughts does your future ideal body think about food, exercise, self-image, etc.?

_____

_____

_____

_____

_____

_____

_____

_____

_____

_____

Game 18

THE SCULPTURE GAME

❖

Upon touching sand, may it turn to gold.

— GREEK PROVERB

This game involves imagining the feelings you would experience if you had your ideal figure. If you have a strong
connection to your sense of touch, this game will be helpful.

Close your eyes. Put your arms in front of you and vividly
imagine touching a sculpture of yourself with your ideal body. If
you are feeling your body thinner, feel the details of your slender
face, your well-defined cheekbones. Feel your arms thinner or
more toned, feel your hip bones. If you want to manifest more
muscles, imagine feeling your toned biceps and your strong
legs. Feel your curves and angles, as if you were really touching
them right now. What does it feel like? Feel the skin across your
stomach, your chest, your neck. Do this long enough until you
feel a very real emotional response. Hold on to this feeling for
as long as you can.

If you are creative you may even want to buy some clay and sculpt your ideal body. Remember to have fun with this. It doesn't have to be a masterpiece; it just has to help you get into the feeling place of having the body you desire.

Game 19

BODY IMAGING GAME

❖

In order to change the printout of the body, we
must learn to rewrite the software of the mind.

—Deepak Chopra, M.D.

Make copies of photographs of your face. Cut out your face
from the photographs and set them aside. Next, cut out
images of people who already have the body of your dreams from
magazines, or print them out from the Internet. Paste your face
over the faces of these people. This is a fun exercise to get you
to visualize what it would look like for you to be living in your
dream body now. Now put these pictures in a place where you
can look at them every day. They could be on your fridge, in your
closet, or possibly on the mirror in your bathroom. Looking at
these images daily will help you to imagine what it would feel like
to already be living in the body of your dreams. This will help you
attract the means to easily make your dream a reality.

Game 20

WHY DO I WANT IT?

❖

People often say that motivation doesn't last.
Well neither does bathing—that's why we
recommend it daily.

—ZIG ZIGLAR

Write out twenty reasons why you want your ideal body. For example, you might want it so that you can shop for more stylish clothes. You might want it so that you feel more confident socially, at work, with your friends, or with a potential romantic partner.

List your reasons, and experience the vibration you'd feel if you already had your ideal body.

Why I want my ideal body

1. _____

_____

2. _____

_____

3. _____

_____

4. _____

_____

5. _____

_____

6. _____

_____

7. _____

_____

8. _____

_____

9. _____

_____

10. _____

_____

11. _____

_____

12. _____

_____

13. _____

_____

14. _____

_____

15. _____

_____

16. _____

_____

17. _____

_____

18. _____

_____

19. _____

_____

20. _____

_____

Whenever you focus on the "whys" of your desires, you attract them to you.

Games to Create Career Success

Game 21

THE INTERVIEW

❖

If you want a quality, act as if you already had it.

— WILLIAM JAMES

This is a wonderful exercise to help you to really talk, think, and feel as if the desire is already yours. This game requires at least two people; one is the "Interviewer" and the other is the "Interviewee." Basically the two of you create a fictional interview based on the interviewee having *already* achieved their desire. For instance, if your desire is to be a famous actor, you could have your "talk show host" interview you by asking you questions about how you like being famous. If your desire is to win the megalotto, then you could have your interviewer ask you questions about what it's like to be rich. If your desire is to find true love, your interviewer could ask you what it's like to have this amazing relationship. If your desire is to heal from an illness, have the interviewer ask you questions about the healing.

This game is very effective if the "interviewer" asks very specific questions and can continue to ask questions that keep you in the feeling place of already having the desire.

This is supposed to be fun, but do your best to stay as serious as possible during the "interview" so that you'll start to feel the buzz of joy that accompanies the feeling place of already having your desire.

Here are some sample questions:

1. So how does it feel now that this has happened to you?
2. Do you feel different than before?
3. How would you describe your new life?
4. How is it different from how it was before?
5. What would you tell someone who wants to achieve this same desire?
6. How do you see the world, now that this is your life?

Game 22

EXPECTING SUCCESS

⋅⋅⋅⋄⋅⋅⋅

*It is better to light one candle than
to curse the darkness.*

—CHINESE PROVERB

Our positive beliefs about what is possible for our careers
help to create success, but our negative beliefs block our
career desires from manifesting. We therefore must find ways
to strengthen our positive beliefs regarding our life's work and
align them with our desires. This exercise helps us "get out of
the Universe's way," by allowing it to work its magic for creating career success. Think of your dream career situation. Write
the dream that you desire here:

Desire: _____

_____

_____

_____

Write twenty reasons why you know you will attain this dream career. You may want to include reasons acknowledging the magical nature of the Universe. Recognize the Power that created the stars, moons, flowers, babies, and you. Include past accomplishments, your skills or other career desires that have already manifested for you, or how others have achieved similar things. These reasons should make you feel good. List them here:

1. _____

_____

2. _____

_____

3. _____

_____

4. _____

_____

5. _____

_____

6. _____

_____

7. _____

_____

8. _____

_____

9. _____

_____

10. _____

_____

11. _____

_____

12. _____

_____

13. _____

_____

14. _____

_____

15. _____

_____

16. _____

_____

17. _____

_____

18. _____

_____

19. _____

_____

20. _____

_____

These reasons, positive expectations, and beliefs are your best friends in terms of opening yourself up to succeeding at your life's passion. Read them aloud three times in a row daily for thirty days, or record them on a tape recorder and listen to the tape once a day for thirty days. Doing this will ingrain these beliefs into your vibration. From there, you will easily attract the right people, places, situations, and ideas into your life for manifesting your perfect career.

Game 23

GETTING INTO CHARACTER

❖❖❖

I love acting. It's so much more real than life.

—OSCAR WILDE

Since I have a theater background I have often used this game to help me lucidly understand how it would feel to have my desires. It is common for many performers to stay in character even when the cameras aren't rolling, or backstage between scenes. They do this because they think their performance will be stronger by being consistent. They try to think the thoughts of their character, to feel the feelings of their character, to walk and talk as their character, so that they may breathe life into the character.

With this game we are going to pretend that we are a master thespian/actor who is taking on the role of a lifetime. We are playing the part of the person who has already achieved total career success. For instance, if you want to be a successful author, you will now play the role of an international bestselling writer. If you want to be a veterinarian, you will now play the role of a revered animal doctor. If you want to open your own restaurant, you will now play the part of a successful restaurateur.

How does your character feel?

What thoughts does your character think?

How does your character walk and talk?

What are your character's hopes and fears?

How does it feel to embody this character fully?

Describe below what it's like to be this character:

_____

_____

_____

_____

_____

_____

_____

Throughout the day, stay in character as much as possible. Breathe life into your character. Make it as real as possible so that you know exactly how it feels to have this dream come true.

Game 24

TAKE STOCK OF
YOUR ASSETS

❖

*Always bear in mind that your own resolution to
succeed is more important than any other one thing.*

— ABRAHAM LINCOLN

How do we expect anyone else to believe in us if we don't believe in ourselves? If we don't value ourselves professionally, we are sending out the signal to others that we don't deserve great success or that we're not confident enough to perform well. This exercise is the confidence builder we need to realize all that we truly have to offer.

Make a list of at least twenty of your skills, assets, qualities, and personality traits that make you a winner professionally.

For example:

1. I am always on time.
2. I am funny and tell great jokes.
3. I am very savvy with numbers.
4. I thrive in a crisis.

Your turn.

My assets:

1. _____
2. _____
3. _____
4. _____
5. _____
6. _____
7. _____
8. _____
9. _____
10. _____
11. _____
12. _____
13. _____
14. _____
15. _____
16. _____
17. _____
18. _____
19. _____
20. _____

Now read this list daily and add new items often.

Games to Create
Objects/Things You Desire

Game 25

10 IN 1 APPRECIATION

❖

There are only two ways to live . . . one is
as though nothing is a miracle . . . the other is
as if everything is.

— ALBERT EINSTEIN

As we begin to vibrate at the frequency of APPRECIATION, we attract into our lives more things to be appreciative of. Focusing on ten things that we appreciate about one thing trains us to be skilled appreciators and turns our dominant vibration into a vibration of gratitude.

Here's how this exercise works. Choose something in life you appreciate. Now list the things you appreciate about this one thing. For instance, you could say:

I appreciate my bed.

1. I appreciate the pillow top softness.
2. I appreciate the sturdiness of the frame.
3. I appreciate how big the headboard and sideboards make it feel.
4. I appreciate the ornate decoration of the bed.
5. I appreciate how comfortable the sheets are.
6. I appreciate how perfect my pillow is.
7. I appreciate how warm I feel under the blanket, yet it's breathable.
8. I appreciate that my spouse is in it.
9. I appreciate that it smells clean and fresh.
10. I appreciate the size of the mattress.

As you learn to focus appreciation energy deeply into one thing, your attraction becomes like a laser, vibrating at a high, fast level of appreciation.

Many of my clients have reported that this exercise often infuses a sense of well-being into the object on which they focus. Intensely focused vibrations of love may cause plants to come back to life. Your electronics may work better. Your pet may become happier.

Appreciating many different things is a great exercise, too. But focusing on ten things that you like about one object trains your mind to focus on one thing long enough to evoke profound feelings of gratitude, thereby attracting more things into your life to feel grateful for.

I appreciate _____.
(Now list ten things you appreciate about this item.)

  1. I appreciate _____

  2. I appreciate _____

  3. I appreciate _____

  4. I appreciate _____

  5. I appreciate _____

  6. I appreciate _____

  7. I appreciate _____

  8. I appreciate _____

  9. I appreciate _____

10. I appreciate _____

Game 26

WHAT I REALLY WANT

❖

Sounds of the wind or sounds of the sea
Make me happy just to be.

—JUNE POLIS

Ask yourself: Why do I want certain objects? If I could have all the things I want, but not have any of the positive emotions about them when I received them, would I still want them?

If you are honest with yourself, you will answer no. You want these things because of the way you think they will make you feel. That is the essence of your desires. If that's the case, why not make the associated emotions your primary goal?

For instance, if you want a brand-new car, it's probably because you want to feel one or more of the following emotions:

luxurious
safe

secure

free

exhilarated

peaceful

content

wealthy

beautiful

refined

Write down your "feeling" goals. Think regularly about every feeling you want to have.

For example:

I feel wealthy.

I feel glamorous.

I feel blessed.

I feel talented.

I feel powerful.

I feel beautiful.

I feel sexy.

I feel rich.

I feel loving.

I feel loved.

I feel connected.

I feel opulent.

I feel inspired.

Your turn:

I feel _____.

I feel _____.

I feel _____.

I feel _____.

I feel _____.

I feel _____.

I feel _____.

I feel _____.

I feel _____.

I feel _____.

For reinforcement, record your voice saying each of these feelings and desires three times. For example, record "I feel wealthy. I feel wealthy. I feel wealthy," then move on to the next. Then listen to these statements when you first wake up in the morning and when you are falling asleep at night.

As these exercises help you attract more good feelings, you will begin to attract the outer forms to reflect these inner feelings, such as the new car you want.

Game 27

I'LL TAKE ONE OF
THOSE, PLEASE

❖

If the only prayer you ever say
in life is "thank you" . . . that
is enough.

— MEISTER ECKHART

This is the game I use most for attracting physical objects into my life. I appreciate every nuance of the object before it gets here. If you want a new car, appreciate the new car smell, the sense of luxury and safety, the handling, the speed, the beauty, and the sound system. Appreciate every appealing detail, and then say to the Universe, "I'll take one of those, please."

Identify two physical objects that you desire and write the many things you appreciate about those desires. List the aspects of these desires that will cause you to feel appreciation.

Desire #1   Desire #2

Aspects   *Aspects*

1. _____   1. _____

   _____   _____

2. _____   2. _____

   _____   _____

3. _____   3. _____

   _____   _____

4. _____   4. _____

   _____   _____

5. _____   5. _____

   _____   _____

If you find yourself thinking thoughts like "Yes, but it's not here yet," or "It will never come to me," you need to refocus your attention on the aspects of the desire you appreciate. Then say aloud to the Universe, "I'll take one of those, please."

This exercise seems simple, but it is one of the most powerful games for attracting specific desires.

Game 28

THE IMMERSION GAME

⋯⋄⋯

Imagination is everything. It is the preview
of life's coming attractions.

— ALBERT EINSTEIN

How many times have you gone into a fancy restaurant and, just by being there, felt a little more abundant? Or by trying on that beautiful designer dress, you felt wealthier? Or by visiting an art museum, felt a bit more creative? The outer world can act like a prop to help us feel wealthy, healthy, successful, romantically cherished, etc. Instead of reacting to the outer world's changing conditions like a flame in the wind, we instead can utilize the physical world to help us feel our desires as being real.

Here's how.

Pick one of your desires, for example, to own a new car or home. Now, just for fun, call up the car dealer and request the buyer's guide for the car. Even better, go to the car dealer and test-drive the car for the afternoon. By doing this, you are activating the feelings of actually owning the car, which sends the signal to the Universe that the car is already yours or that you are truly prepared to buy a new car, thus attracting it to you.

Do the same thing if you want to purchase your dream home. Most real estate agencies have open houses at least one day a week. Next Sunday (or whenever there is an open house in your desired area) go visit the home and act as if you're really interested in buying it (because you are!). You will activate all the same feelings of someone who is actually looking for a home and has the money to buy it. The Internet is also wonderful for this because many homes for sale have online virtual tours and detailed information so you can easily immerse yourself into your desire.

If you want a new wardrobe, go window-shopping and only look at clothing you most want to wear. Imagine purchasing everything you want without hesitation.

Now it's your turn:

List a desire: _____

Outline some ways you can live out this desire: _____

_____

_____

_____

_____

_____

_____

_____

_____

Now go do all or some of the things you've just listed.

Using the outer world to stimulate our imaginations sends out a very clear signal to the Universe that we already have the thing we want, and when that happens, we very quickly manifest the desire.

Games to Create More Self-Love

Game 29

I LOVE ME

❖

I don't like myself. I'm crazy about myself.

— MAE WEST

Self-love is one of the most important vibrations we can radiate out to the world. When we love ourselves, we vibrate at worthiness, entitlement, and deservingness, and then attract back situations, people, ideas, feelings, and circumstances that match our self-love. When we don't love ourselves, it is as if we are sending out a vibrational "Kick me" sign to the Universe, by saying, "I don't value me, so why should anyone/anything out there value me?" For this reason, it is so important that we learn to love, respect, value, and appreciate ourselves deeply and sincerely. People often tell me, "I want to love myself but I don't know how." Here is a fun and easy game for practicing the art of self-love.

Buy a notebook/journal and write on the front, HOW DO I LOVE ME? LET ME COUNT THE WAYS.

Every day, for thirty days, list ten or more things you like, love, enjoy, value, respect, or appreciate about yourself.

For example, day one may be something like:

1. I love my toes.

2. I appreciate how kind I am.

3. I value what a good friend I am.

4. I like my hair.

5. I love that I am a part of the Universe.

6. I enjoy my own company.

7. I respect how well spoken I am.

8. I love that I play the cello.

9. I love what a cute baby I was.

10. I like that I make people laugh.

Your ten things:

1. I love my _____

2. I love that I'm _____

3. I value my ability to _____

4. I respect my _____

5. I appreciate my _____

6. I like my _____

7. I like that I am _____

8. I love my _____

9. I love that I _____

10. I appreciate that I'm _____

After listing the ten things you love about yourself, now list three things you can do for yourself today to *show* yourself how much you love and value yourself.

For example:

    1. Today I am going to read a good book.

    2. Today I'm going to eat fresh vegetables.

    3. Today I'm going to take a long bath.

Your three things:

    1. Today I am going to _____

    2. Today I am going to _____

    3. Today I am going to _____

By noticing what we love about ourselves, we will attract more self-love and love from the outer world. By taking the time to actively give to ourselves, we are sending out a clear signal to the Universe that we deserve the best. The outer world will appear to value us more because we are valuing ourselves.

Game 30

HOTTER-COLDER

❖

*A man is a success if he gets up in the morning
and goes to bed at night and in between does
what he wants to do.*

— BOB DYLAN

When you were a child, did you ever play "hotter-colder"?
Someone would hide an object and let you know how
close you were by saying "hotter" (meaning you were close to the
object) or "colder" (meaning you were getting farther away).

This exercise is designed to bring your vibration up to the
frequency of joy and awareness of your inner guidance. Playing is simple. All day, for one whole day, make it your goal to
get "hotter" or closer to your desire. When you feel a pleasant
emotion, you're vibrationally matched to your desires. "Colder"
means that you're focusing on something that's not in alignment
with your desires. As you practice, getting "hotter" will become
automatic, and you will begin to develop a highly tuned inner

guidance system. Here are the questions that you should ask yourself during the day:

Does this thought that I'm thinking make me feel good?
If yes, milk it. If not, find a thought that makes you feel better.
Does this action I'm taking feel good?
If yes, do it. If not, do something else.
Do these words I'm about to say feel good?
If yes, say them. If no, say something that feels better.
Does this TV show, this activity, this food, feel good?
If yes, enjoy it. If not, do something else.
Do my thoughts about these people feel good?
If yes, think more of them. If no, think differently about them.

Follow what feels good. Your emotions are your guidance system. Your Higher Self can speak only through you and your body. It knows what you want. Listen to the signals it's giving by paying attention to what feels good and what doesn't. When you do, you'll experience your happiest dreams.

How does that feel?

Game 31

THE PARTY HAS ALREADY STARTED

·⟐·

If half a century of living has taught me
anything at all, it has taught me that nothing
can bring you peace but yourself.

— DALE CARNEGIE

L etting go" does not mean giving up your desire. It means allowing the Law of Attraction to do its job. It handles the "how-tos" while you only handle the "feel goods" and the "what you wants."

Too often we get in the way of the Law of Attraction by thinking that we have to figure out the "how-tos." The Intelligence that created life and stars and babies and planets can darn well figure out your desire if you get out of the way and have some fun already.

Here are two great analogies:

When you use a player piano, you program it and plug it in, but you let it play the songs. If you sit down and try to play along, you get in the way of the beautiful music. Your job is simply to plug it in and turn it on. Connect to Source by finding ways to feel good. Next, tell it what song to play—tell Source your desires. Then sit back and enjoy the show.

When a woman gets pregnant, she doesn't have to go to medical school to study anatomy and molecular physics in order to make the baby's tiny toes and fingers and head and heart. She just feeds herself healthful foods and relaxes, knowing some Intelligence beyond her consciousness is creating this baby. That's how we need to be with ALL our desires.

1. Decide what you want: _____

_____

2. Feed yourself good thoughts about the desire: (For example: I am seeing signs everywhere that my desire is right around the corner. I feel good about my desire most of the time. Playing the games in this book really helps me feel good about my desire before it gets here, and those feelings are what it is all about, etc.) _____

_____

_____

_____

_____

_____

3. Relax and have fun; expect it to come to you at the divine right time.

If you could get out of your own way, relax, and have fun, all the desires you have lined up outside your doorstep would start to pour in. Every time you check to see if it's here yet, you push it further away. Instead, say, "I'm going to make my present moment so much fun, it won't matter when 'it' gets here." And *voilà*, it will arrive.

Today, what desire can you get out of the way of? Try your best to fill your "fun tank" and live as if the party has already started.

Do three things today for just plain fun to show the Universe you trust that it has your desires under control and you can relax. Now list what you've done for yourself.

For example:

1. I took a bath and gave myself a facial.
2. I went to my favorite café and got a latte.
3. I bought myself a dozen roses.

What you did for yourself today:

1. _____

_____

2. _____

_____

3. _____

_____

After you do each thing, say to the Universe, "The more I relax and have fun, the faster my desires come to me. I trust that the Universe will deliver."

Game 32

MAGIC FEEL GOOD

---❖---

The landscape belongs to the person
who looks at it.

—RALPH WALDO EMERSON

Pick ten things to do for sheer pleasure and declare it "Magical Feel-Good Day." Here are some examples:

Eat strawberries in the sunshine.

Play with your pet.

Act like the party of your life has already started.

Cry from joy about how much you love someone.

Hold a baby.

Do an act of kindness for someone . . . just because.

Sit in a hot tub under the stars.

Say a prayer of gratitude for the dollars in your bank account.

Really hear someone when s/he shows appreciation to you.

Say "thank you" all day long . . . and mean it.

Go for a walk by a lake with your dog.

Snuggle on a couch and watch a movie.

Let go and trust that the Universe loves you.

Grieve over a loss by sobbing from your gut. (Yes, real grief feels good, like relief and love.)

Enjoy a fresh cup of coffee in the morning.

Tell someone how much he or she means to you.

Watch movies intended for little kids.

Work with clay (or Play-Doh).

Take a bubble bath.

Bake blueberry muffins.

Laugh so hard that you can't catch your breath.

Stop and realize how loved you've been in your life.

The key to everything you want is feeling good now. Too simple? It is simple only when you allow yourself to do it. Practice this game today. All you have to do is pick ten things to do for sheer pleasure. Enjoy.

Ten things to do today for sheer pleasure:

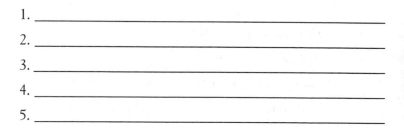

1. _____

2. _____

3. _____

4. _____

5. _____

6. _____
7. _____
8. _____
9. _____
10. _____

Game 33

FILLING YOUR FUN TANK

·❖·

If you want to be creative, stay in part a child, with the creativity and invention that characterizes children before they are deformed by adult society.

—JEAN PIAGET

Have you ever come back from a vacation to discover some problem had worked itself out on its own? This is because you were vibrationally matched to joy while on vacation and you allowed similar energies into your life.

Let's imagine that a "tank" needs to be filled with fun regularly. When the tank is filled, you'll have more to offer to yourself and to others because you'll be naturally vibrating at a higher, happier frequency. So let's fill those fun tanks.

Give yourself permission to do this game every day. Yes, this is an important game to do daily, at least for a little while, until having fun becomes a habit.

Write down a list of all the things you now enjoy, that you've enjoyed in the past, or that you have always wanted to do.

Here are some examples:

Going out to a nice dinner.

Working with clay.

Going ice-skating.

Taking your dog for a walk.

Taking a bath.

Going to the zoo.

Raising homing pigeons.

Learning to crochet.

Write your list here:

_____

_____

_____

_____

_____

_____

_____

_____

_____

_____

_____

_____

Regularly add your new ideas to the list. Here's the fun part. Start by doing at least three of these things each week, and build up to doing one each day. Some of them can be small, like walking your dog or taking a bath, but try to include a big one, at least one, each week.

Now go have some fun.

Games to Create True Love/ Your Perfect Mate

Game 34

MORNING AND BEDTIME STORIES: MY FAIRY-TALE HAPPY ENDING

❖

Life itself is the most wonderful fairy tale.

—HANS CHRISTIAN ANDERSON

How many of you loved to have stories read to you as a child? Children's minds are open, receptive, and believing. When we are children we allow love to pour through us because we haven't yet learned to resist it. As adults, our minds are their most childlike when we are sleepy or in deep meditation. At these times, our minds are the most receptive, impressionable, allowing, and faith filled. The conscious mind becomes a little toned down, and our subconscious mind is receptive to taking "commands." (See I Command . . . , page 217.)

For this exercise, you will need a small tape recorder. I use a handheld version.

Write out a script from your most ideal romantic fairy-tale future, complete with a happy ending. Perhaps you could write about a perfect day in your future romantic life. Include information about what your romantic partner looks and acts like, how you treat each other, your mutual interests, emotional happiness, romance, spirituality—whatever is most important to you. Write in the past tense, as if your true-love relationship has already manifested and you are reading the story to yourself.

Now record the story into your tape recorder, in your natural voice. Make sure the script would really make you happy. Every morning for thirty days, stay in bed ten minutes longer than usual, and listen to your tape. While you are still sleepy, let yourself imagine how the story would make you feel if it came true.

This game will bring your dominant vibration to the frequency of "already having true love." When you go to bed at night, play the tape again. As you are getting very sleepy, listen to the tape, like a bedtime story being told to you about your perfect romance. If you do this regularly, you may start to dream about this vision as though it's already happening. This is a sign that the Law of Attraction is already starting to work and you are opening up to your desires. Sweet dreams.

My happy-ending story (be sure to use more paper or use your own journal for more space):

Game 35

YOU HAVE LOVE NOW

❖

What a wonderful life I've had. I only
wish I had realized it sooner.

— COLETTE

This is a great game for creating more love in your life by realizing the ways in which you already have and enjoy the essence of love now.

Decide on what you desire in a loving relationship. Describe the emotions you think you would feel if you already had this relationship. For example:

Desire: To Meet My Soul Mate

1. I would feel happiness.
2. I would feel attractive.
3. I would feel loved.
4. I would feel connected.
5. I would feel companionship.

Describe the areas of your life where you already feel these emotions. For example:

1. I already feel happiness about:
   a. My health.

  b. My great friendships.

  c. My car.

 2. I already feel attractive:

  a. When I wear my blue dress.

  b. After a facial.

Your turn:

  Your true-love desire: _____

  Now, list five emotions you would have if you already possessed this desire:

  1. _____

  2. _____

  3. _____

  4. _____

  5. _____

Using the corresponding spaces, give three examples of where you already feel these emotions.

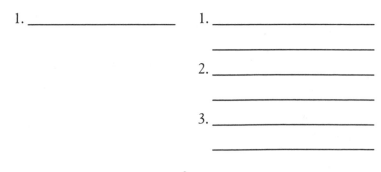

2. _____

                   1. _____

                   _____

                   2. _____

                   _____

                   3. _____

                   _____

3. _____

                   1. _____

                   _____

                   2. _____

                   _____

                   3. _____

                   _____

4. _____

                   1. _____

                   _____

                   2. _____

                   _____

                   3. _____

                   _____

5. _____

                   1. _____

                   _____

                   2. _____

                   _____

                   3. _____

                   _____

Game 36

MY PERFECT MATE IN DETAIL

⋯⋄⋯

Love doesn't just sit there like a stone;
it has to be made — like bread, remade
all the time, made new.

— URSULA K. LE GUIN

Write out a list of every quality you can think of to describe the perfect mate for you. The longer and more specific the list, the better. This helps to make your desired relationship feel more tangible and will send out a very specific request to the Universe. Start with fifty qualities, both internal and external, that you are looking for in your ideal mate. Then add to them often, refining your vision down to the last detail.

Remember to include how he/she makes you feel. Also, it is best to play this game without any specific person in mind. Just include details about your dream partner. If a certain person has qualities you are looking for in a mate, you can list the person in that regard. For example, "They are very much a gentleman, opening doors for me, etc., like David was." Include everything, from physical attributes to hobbies and quirky traits. Read your list to yourself often until you can deeply resonate with the feelings of already having him/her in your life. You'll be amazed at how many of these details your future partner will embody!

Game 37

LOVER'S HIGH

❖

The best love is the kind that awakens the soul and
makes us reach for more, that plants a fire in our
hearts and brings peace to our minds.

—NOAH TO ALLIE IN *THE NOTEBOOK*

This is a fun game to play to get into the feeling place of true love and romantic happiness. Over a month, make a commitment to rent some of the most romantic films you can find. As you watch these films, match your frequency to the feelings of the couple in love for the full length of the movie.

Do this as often as you can. For this month, stay away from depressing movies, books, or magazine articles about failed romance and just settle your mind, emotions, and vibrations on beautiful love stories with happy endings.

Here is a possible list of films to rent. (Remember to find your own as well. What may be romantic to one person could be unappealing to another.)

1. *Sleepless in Seattle*
2. *Must Love Dogs*
3. *Moonstruck*
4. *Pride and Prejudice*
5. *Bridget Jones's Diary*
6. *Somewhere in Time*
7. *Lady and the Tramp*
8. *The Notebook*
9. *Notting Hill*
10. *Desk Set*
11. *Serendipity*
12. *Say Anything*
13. *Ever After*
14. *Sabrina*
15. *Pretty Woman*
16. *It Happened One Night*
17. *Houseboat*
18. *An Affair to Remember*
19. *50 First Dates*
20. *When Harry Met Sally . . .*

Games to Create Spiritual Connection / Inner Peace

Game 38

QUIET YOUR MIND

⁙

*Learn to get in touch with the silence within
yourself and know that everything in this life has a
purpose, there are no mistakes, no coincidences, all
events are blessings given to us to learn from.*

— ELISABETH KÜBLER-ROSS

If you quiet your mind you will glide into a stream of pure,
high-vibrating energy and will easily enter into an allowing
mode. There are an infinite number of ways to quiet your mind.

Experiment with different methods to achieve this so that
you can get into the mode of allowing in your desires. First
ask yourself, "Am I predominantly a physical person, a more

intellectual person, or am I more emotional?" Don't think too much about the answer. Start with the first thing that comes to you.

If you are a physically oriented person, put on some music, preferably something you really like, dim the lights, and start moving your body with the music. There is no right way to do this. Just allow your body and the music to merge as one and enjoy the ride. Do this for ten to twenty minutes. Voilà! You have just quieted your mind. Do this as often as you want.

If you are more intellectual, sit quietly and close your eyes, then imagine your thoughts as leaves on a stream. Instead of following the thought stream, simply observe them.

When the first thought comes to you, say, "I'm having a thought about _____ ."

Then when the next thought comes along, observe that one.

Let each thought drift out of sight. This neutral observer of your thoughts is you as Spirit, pure high-vibrating energy. It is you not thinking in words, but rather just being awareness. This is a wonderful exercise for people who feel like they "think too much."

If you are an emotionally inclined person, sit quietly in a room and breathe in for a count of five while imagining the love of the Universe entering through the top of your head. Then breathe out to a count of five, imagining the same love pouring out of your heart to all the beings of the world. Do this exercise for ten to twenty minutes, or however long you feel inclined.

As you progress, you may try other emotionally, physically, or intellectually oriented techniques. There are no right or wrong methods here, just fun ways for you to quiet your mind so that you can resonate at a naturally high frequency of bliss.

Game 39

UNCONDITIONAL LOVE

❖

*There is more hunger for love and appreciation
in this world than for bread.*

— MOTHER TERESA

This game teaches you the important benefit of being able
to love unconditionally. You'll learn how to stay connected to your well-being, no matter how anyone treats you.

This includes individuals who seem to have a problem with you. Remember, if they are judging you, they are simply dealing with their own issues, which have nothing to do with you. Only you can decide how you are going to feel about another's behavior, and you can choose to vibrate at love and compassion for both of you.

Let's build an unconditional love muscle. Think of someone in your life who challenges your sense of well-being. Ask yourself, "How do I feel when I think of this person?" Perhaps you feel hurt, angry, or jealous. Now say a mental "thank-you" to that person for giving you practice in staying connected to your well-being in all circumstances. This person is your teacher. If you can learn to feel grateful for this person's presence in your life, you'll soften your vibration toward that person.

Now take a few minutes and list ten things about this person that you appreciate. For example:

He is kind to animals.
He is generous with his money.
She laughs at my jokes.

If you have a personal relationship with this individual, list three memories you share that are uplifting (similar to Life Touchstones, page 225).

For example: When we were kids, we rode tandem bikes at the beach.

The shift in focus will remind you of the truth about this person—how much you love him/her, and how much s/he loves you. Practice this exercise every day until there's a softening or a shift in the way you feel about the person. You will start to notice a predominant shift in your vibration, and that person may begin to shift toward you as well.

Practice this exercise for anything and anyone, including institutions, organizations, and even your government.

Game 40

GIVING LOVE ALL DAY

❖

The heart that is generous and kind
most resembles God.

— Robert Burns

The night before you play this game, make a commitment that for all of the following day you will give love to everyone you come in contact with. This means that, for example, you will only compliment your spouse, only give love and encouragement to your children, give lots of hugs and kisses to your pets, give way to others in traffic, give five dollars to a person in need. Call someone and say how much s/he means to you. Write your mother a letter of appreciation. Give yourself a bubble bath and speak loving words into a mirror.

This is a vibrationally uplifting game with addiction potential and may become a permanent part of your lifestyle. As you give, you are also telling the Universe that you already have a lot and are overflowing. As a result, what you give will come back to you tenfold.

We are love, poured into bodies. Living love is our natural state. Give love all day long to yourself and to others and watch your life blossom.

Game 41

VISIT YOUR FUTURE SELF

❖

*There is nothing like returning to a place that
remains unchanged to find the ways in which you
yourself have altered.*

—NELSON MANDELA

According to quantum physics, all possible realities are unfolding in infinite dimensions right now. This includes
the reality of already having all your desires. Right now, there is
a version of "You" who is wealthy, healthy, happy, in love, and
enlightened, and has whatever you desire. This game helps you
find that "You" who is currently living in that reality so that
you can understand the way that "You" thinks. This will allow
you to become more like that version of yourself who is already
living all your dreams.

For this exercise, sit in a chair or lie down and close your
eyes. Listen to the sounds around you, and then just become
aware of your breathing for a couple of minutes. Really settle
into the present moment.

Now imagine that there's a long hallway, and at the end of this long hallway is the "You" who already has the thing, person, or emotional state you are wanting. This "You" is already living your dream.

Walk down the hall toward "yourself." What does this "You" look like as you approach? What is this "You" wearing? Does this "You" seem calm and relaxed? Are "You" smiling? Take a minute and describe what "You" look and feel like.

_____

_____

_____

_____

_____

_____

_____

Now take your future "You" by the hand and exit through a door to the outside world. See the beautiful natural scenery around you. It could be a lake or ocean or forest. Now lead your future "You" by the hand to a nearby bench and sit down. Look into "your" eyes and then proceed to ask your "Future Self" the following questions:

1. What do I most need to know to create my desires?

Your Future Self's answer: _____

_____

_____

_____

_____

_____

2. What does it feel like to have these desires fulfilled?

   Your Future Self's answer: _____

_____

_____

_____

_____

_____

Now give your future self a hug and imagine merging vibrationally with this "You" who has already realized your desires. Open your eyes, take a deep breath, and truly embody your future self now.

Game 42

WHO ELSE IS GOING TO BENEFIT?

∙❖∙

Life is a gift, and it offers us the privilege,
opportunity, and responsibility to give something
back by becoming more.

— ANTHONY ROBBINS

One of the best ways to let yourself have your desires is to think about all the people you will serve by manifesting your dreams. We don't live in a vacuum, and the most practical way we can help others is by being happy, healthy, and abundant ourselves. When you are happy it is easier for others to be happy when they are around you. When you are healthy you have more energy to help others. When you are wealthy, you have more financial resources available to aid others. The better off you are, the more you have to give to the world. So if up until now you have felt that feeling it real is selfish, self-centered, or greedy, you might want to think again. By looking deeply at all the people you will help by manifesting your desires, you will give yourself even more permission to let in the good.

Let's start by thinking about someone you've helped as a result of your good fortune. Say you received a massage today that was calming and de-stressing. When dealing with your children later, your calm attitude may have helped you to listen attentively to them or stay calm while they were quarreling. Your massage also helped the masseuse financially. Your massage may have also helped your spouse or significant other to relax after work because of your good mood.

Let's think of the ways that you having your desires will serve others.

My desire: _____

_____

All the ways that my having my desire will help others:

1. _____
2. _____
3. _____
4. _____
5. _____
6. _____
7. _____
8. _____

9. _____

10. _____

It will be such a good thing for the world when your dreams come true!

Game 43

THE SECRET GIVER

❖

One act of beneficence, one act of
real usefulness, is worth all the abstract
sentiment in the world.

— ANN RADCLIFFE

I came up with this game after I heard the story of how one famous talk show host sometimes pays the toll for several cars behind her at a toll bridge. This gave me goose bumps as I realized how good that must feel for her to do something that kind. There's something very rewarding about you being the only one who knows about the kind act you've done for another. This isn't to say that it isn't also fun to give to others when they know you're the giver. That's a lot of fun, too! But being a secret giver has a special uplifting quality about it.

So try it today: do something kind for someone who will never know that it was you who did it.

Here are some possible ideas:

1. Pay for the person's food behind you in line at the drive-through.
2. Send a card and money with no return address to someone you value or appreciate.
3. Write an anonymous note of appreciation on a Web site's guestbook.
4. Wash someone's windshield in a parking lot.
5. Write an anonymous letter to the editor of your newspaper praising a local restaurant/person/company.

Come up with your own ideas. Doing one of these a day can really lift your spirits and cause you to feel very abundant because you are giving so much!

Games to Create Health and Wellness

Game 44

WHAT'S HEALTHY NOW?

❖

The greatest wealth is health.

— VIRGIL

When we are faced with a health challenge, it's hard not to be intensely focused on the part of our body that is out of balance. We know that the Law of Attraction gives us more of whatever we focus on, so it's important to get our minds off of what's wrong with our body and focus on what is working—what is already healthy.

Every day for the next thirty days, write out at least ten appreciations for those things that are healthy about your body right now. As your dominant vibration shifts toward the health that already exists within you, you will attract more and more health.

For example:

1. I appreciate my sense of vision being so excellent.
2. I appreciate my sense of hearing being so clear.

3. I appreciate that my digestion functions so well.

4. I appreciate that my legs are healthy and I can walk.

How my body is already healthy:

1. I appreciate my _____

2. I appreciate my _____

3. I appreciate my _____

4. I appreciate my _____

5. I appreciate my _____

6. I appreciate my _____

7. I appreciate my _____

8. I appreciate my _____

9. I appreciate my _____

10. I appreciate my _____

Game 45

STORIES OF HEALING

❖

The human body experiences a powerful
gravitational pull in the direction of hope.
That is why the patient's hopes are the
physician's secret weapon. They are the hidden
ingredients in any prescription.

— NORMAN COUSINS

A powerful tool for healing our body is to believe that we can. One of the greatest ways to believe we can heal is by seeking and finding real life stories of others' healings.

For this game, we will need to do a little research. It will take a little bit of effort, but it will be worth it.

Every day, for about ten minutes, seek out stories of people who have healed their bodies. It is helpful, but not imperative, that these people healed from the same issue you are experiencing. An easy way to research healings online is to enter "healed from (enter your body issue)" on a search engine. You can also look in books or find articles in health magazines or online journals, or ask a health specialist. It might also be fun to find quotes about healing and put them up around your house to remind you of the power that your mind has to heal your body.

As you practice this game, you will shift your beliefs toward understanding that your mind can indeed heal your body. So, immerse yourself in reading health success stories, and you, too, will become one of them!

Game 46

REASONS FOR PHYSICAL WELL-BEING

❖

If anything is sacred the human body is sacred.

— WALT WHITMAN

Once you get really clear about why you want physical wellness, you can more easily access ideas and methods for achieving this desired state.

Why do you want to have perfect health?

Think of at least twenty reasons why you would want to feel physically well. For example:

1. I want to live to see my grandchildren.

2. I want to have more energy for my children.

3. I want to be able to run and play on the beach this summer.

List at least twenty reasons, big and small:

1. I want _____

   _____

2. I want _____

   _____

3. I want _____

_____

4. I want _____

_____

5. I want _____

_____

6. I want _____

_____

7. I want _____

_____

8. I want _____

_____

9. I want _____

_____

10. I want _____

_____

11. I want _____

_____

12. I want _____

_____

13. I want _____

_____

14. I want _____

_____

15. I want _____

_____

16. I want _____

_____

17. I want _____

_____

18. I want _____

_____

19. I want _____

_____

20. I want _____

_____

Now read and reread your list every day, coming up with new reasons as often as possible.

Game 47

JOURNALING MY HEALTHY LIFE

❖

Every human being is the author of
his own health or disease.

—SIVANANDA

What would your life look like if you had perfect health? What activities would you participate in that you don't participate in now because of physical limitation? What would your energy level be? How would it affect your relationships, your career, your enthusiasm for living?

In the following space, imagine that you just had a wonderful day living in a perfectly healthy body. Describe what your day was like, what activities you performed, who you spent time with, your energy levels, your accomplishments, etc. Write as if you are writing in your journal at the end of an incredibly active and healthy day.

For example:

JOURNAL ENTRY

What a fun day I just had. . . . I got up this morning at 7 a.m. and went for a jog. The countryside was so beautiful and I felt like I could keep running forever. . . .

Your turn:

JOURNAL ENTRY

_____

_____

_____

_____

_____

_____

_____

Now read this aloud once a day, or record it into your tape player and listen to it once a day.

Quick Pick-me-ups—Games to Jump-start Your Vibration

Game 48

I COMMAND . . .

⋅⋅⋅⋅⋅

The Force both obeys and commands.

— YODA

When we were children, we believed in the power of magic. We believed in our own power to manifest. We hadn't yet learned that our dreams could seem unrealistic or impractical. We were in a state of allowing great belief. Did you ever notice that the kids who truly believed in magic, miracles, and the power of their thoughts to summon the Universe to bring their desires in their dreams, even when it seemed naive to do so, were those who most often grew up to accomplish great things?

This game is for that child inside you who still believes that your words and thoughts are powerful enough to create. It's for the child who still believes in magic, who still feels entitled to all the good things that life has to offer. This exercise will lead you to feel your manifesting power and help you vibrate at POWER, CLARITY, EMPOWERMENT, ENTITLEMENT, DESERVINGNESS, and WORTHINESS.

Here's how it works. It's simple, but powerful. Before the exercise, write out how you feel about your sense of power.

When I think about my sense of power I feel:

_____

_____

_____

_____

Write out ten commands or "orders" that you want the Universe to fulfill for you. By stating the desires in the form of a command, you're letting the Universe know that you're the boss and the Universal Law is meant to serve you. Here are a few examples:

"Universe, I command you to get me fit and toned and slender by summertime."

"Universe, I command you to give me the best-ever relationship with my mother this year."

"Universe, I command you to give me that raise, or an even better form of abundance."

As you do this, you will gradually shift your dominant vibration to empowerment, faith, and trust. The Universe will begin to act in accordance with the words "Your wish is my command." This is a great exercise for those who were taught that wanting was "bad" or who lost their childlike sense that power is born from belief.

List your ten commands for the Universe. Write them down; then—here comes the fun part—grab or make a wand that represents your power. It could be a plastic wand, or one made from tin foil, or even a stick. Decorate it so it reflects your inner child's personality.

With wand in hand, say your commands out loud to the Universe. Then wave your magic wand with authority.

1. Universe, I command you to _____

_____

2. Universe, I command you to _____

_____

3. Universe, I command you to _____

_____

4. Universe, I command you to _____

_____

5. Universe, I command you to _____

_____

6. Universe, I command you to _____

_____

7. Universe, I command you to _____

_____

8. Universe, I command you to _____

_____

9. Universe, I command you to _____

_____

10. Universe, I command you to _____

_____

Notice how you feel after you've given your commands aloud. Write your thoughts down here.

When I think about my sense of power I feel:

_____

_____

_____

_____

_____

The more you practice "commanding" the Universe, the more you set your vibration at empowerment and entitlement, thus attracting to you your desires.

Game 49

GET-HAPPY QUESTIONS

❖

*Be like the bird, who halting in his flight on limb
too slight, feels it give way beneath him, yet sings
knowing he hath wings.*

—VICTOR HUGO

Let's play a game to demonstrate that what you focus on at any given moment is the only thing controlling your mood.

This game is guaranteed to make you feel better now without anything outside of your mental state changing.

Now, answer the questions below:

1. What is the nicest thing anyone has ever done for you?
2. What do you consider your best physical feature (legs, face, toes, etc.)?
3. What do you consider your best personal feature (creativity, kindness, humor, etc.)?

4. If you could choose three memories to carry with you through eternity, what would they be?
5. What's the most enjoyable thing you've ever done?
6. What has been your greatest accomplishment?
7. Who has made you feel the most loved?
8. Look around you. Notice five things that are pleasant, nice, or beautiful.
9. What is the funniest movie you've ever seen?
10. If you knew the Law of Attraction really worked and you could figure out how to master it, what one thing would you like to attract?

See? None of the conditions around you have changed, but you've still been able to change your vibration, your focus, and the things that you are attracting.

Game 50

HA, HA, HA!!!

❖

He who laughs last didn't get it.

—HELEN GIANGREGORIO

Nothing jump-starts a person's vibration the way laughter does. People pay money to go see comedians in order to get that rush that comes from laughing. Author Norman Cousins believes he even healed himself through the power of laughter. Laughing lifts our spirits, improves our moods, and relieves stress. It has been said that laughter is the best medicine. It's also a useful tool for working with the Law of Attraction.

Most people think something funny has to happen in order for them to laugh, but the act of laughing itself can make you want to laugh more.

To prove this theory, try the following. (It's more fun to play this game with someone else, but it's fun alone, too.)

Start out by saying "Ha, ha, ha" pretty loudly. Do this until you feel the genuine urge to keep laughing. It may take ten seconds or it may take a full minute, but eventually you'll naturally want to laugh. Once you feel the genuine urge to laugh, keep laughing as long as possible, and you may find that if you're with someone else, the laughter becomes contagious. It could be the silliness of the exercise or something biological, but either way, you can get yourself to laugh naturally anytime, anyplace. This is a powerful tool. It is an especially effective exercise to use when you are feeling down or when you are upset by something, or taking yourself or someone else too seriously. This game can be used to keep your vibration high and your energy flowing throughout the day.

Game 51

LIFE TOUCHSTONES

We should be careful to get out of an experience
only the wisdom that is in it.

— MARK TWAIN

This is a great game if you are having a hard time getting into a feel-good state and you need a series of thoughts to reconnect you to your well-being. Revisit this game whenever you need a jolt of positivity to remind you of how good life can be. Think of your top ten happiest memories, and describe them in some detail below. If you really feel down, get this book out, mark this page, and reread your top ten touchstones. They are called "touchstones" because these memories help you to quickly access positive emotional vibrations without too much intellectual thought. You can quickly get in "touch" with feelings that have benefited you in the past and will lift your vibration to attract happier thoughts. Here's an example:

1. My mom and I were sitting on the rocks, looking out at the ocean, drinking coffee, and thinking that life doesn't get better than this.

As your touchstones become more familiar, you can use them anytime and anywhere to reconnect to your natural vibration of well-being. This is a great exercise when you need a jolt of happiness.

1. _____

_____

_____

2. _____

_____

_____

3. _____

_____

_____

4. _____

_____

_____

5. _____

_____

_____

6. _____

_____

_____

7. _____

_____

_____

8. _____

_____

_____

9. _____

_____

_____

10. _____

_____

_____

Game 52

DRESSING THE PART

❖

Just around the corner in every woman's
mind—is a lovely dress, a wonderful suit,
or entire costume, which will make an
enchanting new creature of her.

—WILHELA CUSHMAN

When asked how he got into character to play Indiana Jones in the movie *Raiders of the Lost Ark*, Harrison Ford said it was only after he donned his character's fedora hat for the first time that he was able to become Indiana Jones. How we dress does affect our emotional frequency. If we want to feel wealthy but our socks have holes in them, it may be a bit of a challenge to feel it real. If we want to feel beautiful and glamorous but we wear sweatpants all day every day, it may be more difficult to feel it real. Conversely, if we aren't feeling particularly sexy one day, putting on some sexy lingerie may shift our feelings. If we aren't feeling particularly abundant, wearing our fancy watch or shoes may help us to get into the feeling place more easily. If we want to feel creative, we can wear a colorful scarf. If we want to feel like we're famous, we can wear some big sunglasses and a hat. If we want to feel more successful, we can dress in a fancy suit or dress. If we want to feel more active, we can dress in workout gear. Dressing the part, as if we already have the thing we want, helps us to get into the feeling place more easily. If money is an issue, there are wonderful outlet stores and economical clothing stores that carry nice clothes for a great price.

Write down something you want to have. For example: *I want to have a million dollars.*

Now think of how you as a millionaire would dress. Don't think about how someone else would dress, but rather how you would dress. Some millionaires would dress more casually, others more stylishly, others more in business attire. How would *you* as a millionaire dress?

_____

_____

_____

_____

_____

_____

_____

_____

_____

_____

Now find a way to dress that way more often during this coming week. If you have a really nice shirt, wear it, and maybe buying a few more of those shirts will make you feel even more like a millionaire. If you have a watch that always makes you feel abundant, wear that. If you have a dress or shoes or jewelry, wear that. If you don't have anything that makes you feel abundant when you wear it, it's time to go shopping so you can feel it real more easily.

Game 53

TALK TO STRANGERS

⬥⬥⬥

Some stories are true that never happened.

—Elie Wiesel

This game is wonderful for tricking the Universe into thinking you already have your desires. It involves a bit of storytelling, but the great news is that the more you tell these stories, the more likely they are to become real. Don't you love sharing great news? Now you can share the great news before you even get the great news! Here's how it works:

The next time you are talking to a stranger who you may never speak to again (like a telemarketer who calls or a gas station attendant in a town you rarely visit) why not tell them the "great news" of already having achieved your desire? It's a bit like role-playing. When they believe that you are telling the truth, it adds a great deal of energy to your dream and creates a more tangible vibrational signal that is being transmitted out to the Universe. For instance, the next time a telemarketer calls you and asks "How are you doing this evening?" you can answer, "Well, I'm doing VERY WELL! I just got married last week to the man of my dreams and we had the most beautiful honeymoon in Europe!" (Even though you're still single.) Or when you're paying for your gas in that remote town, you could say, "With the price of gas these days, it's a good thing I'm so rich! Luckily I became a multimillionaire last year when my business really took off."

Talking to these people *as if* the dream has already manifested will powerfully assist you in getting into the feeling place as if it already has happened, thus magnetizing the desire to you.

I first learned of the power of this game when I heard that three different lottery winners from different cities who had used a version of this technique were going around telling everyone that they had won a million dollars three weeks *before* they actually won the exact amount of one million dollars!

Our words are very powerful. And if you are intent on "telling the truth," you might ask yourself, what is absolutely true if we create our own reality? Is it the reality that exists around us right now, or the one we are imagining?

Game 54

FAVORITES

⬥⬥⬥

When I'm feeling sad
I simply remember my favorite things.

— RODGERS AND HAMMERSTEIN

This game is a quick way to raise your vibration when you're feeling low and having a case of the "blahs." Answer the following questions as fast as you can. If you want to lift someone else's spirits, ask them these questions.

1. What is your favorite movie?

2. What is your favorite color?

3. Favorite food?

4. Favorite song?

5. Favorite memory?

6. Favorite ice cream flavor?

7. Favorite kisser?

8. Favorite piece of jewelry?

9. Favorite pair of shoes?

10. Favorite comedian?

11. Favorite type of art?

12. Favorite time in history/future?

13. Favorite animal?

14. Favorite bird?

15. Favorite bodily feature?

16. Favorite sound?

17. Favorite way to spend a day?

18. Favorite internal quality?

19. Favorite piece of advice you've ever been given?

20. Favorite hobby?

21. Favorite desire?

22. Favorite quality in a mate?

23. Favorite sport?

24. Favorite place to travel?

25. Favorite type of dancing to watch/dance?

26. Favorite book?

27. Favorite type of cake?

28. Favorite board game?

29. Favorite alcoholic beverage?

30. Favorite nonalcoholic beverage?

31. Favorite author?

Our favorite things make us uniquely us, and the more we focus on what we like, the more we attract things to us that are likable!

Game 55

THE VIBRATIONAL LIBRARY

⋅⟐⋅

Memory is the library of the mind.

—Francis Fauvel Gouraud

We all have memories that evoke certain feelings that we enjoy. This game helps us to remember how certain experiences feel. For instance, we've all had that moment where we first fell in love, and remembering it can easily make us feel the flutter of our heartbeats, the spring in our step, the anticipation of our future together. Whether that relationship had a happy ending or not, we can access specific happy memories within that relationship that help us get into the feeling place we desire now. It's as if we have a vibrational library card and can pick and choose the emotions we are wanting to feel, based on very specific memories.

Here's another example. Say you want to feel wealthy, but right now you have no money in your bank account. More than likely you have at least one memory of a time when money was flowing abundantly. It could be a time when you were a child and didn't have to worry about money. It could be a time when someone gave you a big sum of money. It could be a time when you got a promotion, or an investment paid off. Pick a time when you felt the most carefree and abundant about money. Vividly remember the experience until it evokes a real sense of wealth and abundance within you. Ask yourself, "What did it feel like to have this flow of money in my life?" You can use your vibrational library card at any time, in any place to feel wealthy, healthy, in love, thin, young, successful, creatively fulfilled, peaceful, enlightened, happy, forgiving, joyful. Anything you want.

Game 56

EMOTIONAL GOALS

❖

We are all here for a spell. Get all
the good laughs you can.

— WILL ROGERS

Make a list of the emotions you want to feel over the next twelve months.

To find your emotional goals, ask yourself: If your God said, "I guarantee that all your dreams will come true this year, absolutely," what would you feel?

Here are some examples:

elated
thrilled
relaxed
graced
excited
peaceful
joyful

Now make your list:

1. _____
2. _____
3. _____
4. _____
5. _____
6. _____
7. _____
8. _____
9. _____
10. _____

Take a few of your outer, physical world goals and write them here:

1. _____
2. _____
3. _____
4. _____
5. _____
6. _____
7. _____
8. _____
9. _____
10. _____

You can refer back to these goals often, and remember that focusing on the emotional goals first will naturally help attract the corresponding physical world goals.

Conclusion

We choose our joys and sorrows long
before we experience them.

— KAHLIL GIBRAN

Let's review.

Like frequencies attract like frequencies. All matter is made up of energetic vibration, including our bodies, thoughts, and emotions. Therefore our vibrational thoughts and feelings attract similar vibrational circumstances to themselves. Your feelings also signal whether you're thinking positive or negative thoughts, and thus attracting positive or negative circumstances.

If you feel poor, you attract destitution. If you feel wealthy, you attract wealth. If you feel loved, you attract love from others. If you feel unloved, you attract not being loved from others. The list goes on and on.

The outer world is neutral and reflects the predominant vibrations that you emit. When you look in a mirror, you don't praise or blame the mirror for what you see, because the mirror reflects the image that you project. The Universe works in the same way.

Until we fully embrace responsibility for what we attract into our lives, we'll tend to feel like victims.

We have to stop waiting for the outside world to change if we want to tip the scale toward vibrational frequencies that attract circumstances we enjoy.

Abraham Lincoln said, "People are about as happy as they make up their minds to be." Right now you have a choice. You can focus on all that is already wonderful in your life or you can focus on all that isn't working. The choice you make will determine what you attract. If you choose to look at, analyze, observe, emote, and thus vibrate at what is wrong, you will attract more of that.

It's okay to get angry, sad, depressed, hurt, or frustrated if you realize that these emotions are inner guidance signals that are trying to tell you to think more uplifting thoughts. Or you may have to have a good cry to make you feel better. But if you feel *stuck* in these emotions, you're not listening to them, and you're probably settled into a habitual thought pattern that is wreaking havoc on your circumstances.

If you choose to look at, analyze, observe, emote, and vibrate at what's going right in your life, you will begin to attract more of that. Once this happens, it gets easier and easier to feel good.

Don't get fooled into thinking that the outer good causes your inner feelings. It is *always* your inner feelings that create your outer good. This is why spiritual teachers say, "Don't be attached to things." Those things are just results of how you flow your energy. If it all fell apart tomorrow, you could start to re-create it in an instant through your vibrational power. That's why so many millionaires who lose all their money get it back again. It's a familiar vibration for them to feel rich.

To recap, the most important aspect of the Law of Attraction is getting into the feeling place of already having your desires.

If you can vibrate just 51 percent at the following frequencies, your entire life will transform.

1. love		11.	passion
2. gratitude		12.	creativity
3. appreciation		13.	acceptance
4. wonder		14.	serenity
5. laughter		15.	generosity
6. fun		16.	contribution
7. joy		17.	abundance
8. bliss		18.	wealth
9. peace		19.	energy
10. enthusiasm		20.	health

These are the real riches in life. These emotions are the keys to the kingdom. Nothing in the physical world will ever give you what training yourself to feel these things on a regular basis will give you.

When you feel these emotions, watch the mirror of your life reflect circumstances that match them.

A Final Note

As I write these last lines, my big, old cat, Zorro, rests on my lap, and I am struck by the way his purring feels on my arms. Zorro is one of my great gurus because he says it all without words. I aspire to his appreciation, fascination, acceptance, and love of the present moment. I laugh that I have just written a book about higher frequencies and how to achieve them, when he truly embodies this concept. How I wish he could write this book. If he could, I imagine he would write just two words: Chill out. (Okay, and maybe "tuna fish.")

Even though I'm not as evolved as my Buddha kitty, I have written this book to spread a similar message. I aim to teach the art of emotional mastery so your life can become more peaceful, more content, more passionate, and more joyful. I have provided tools so that you can have more appreciation, fascination, acceptance, and love of the present moment, just like Zorro.

Remember, feeling joy and having fun really are the meaning of life. Enjoy.

My Wins

List below any manifestations you have created while reading this book. These can be big ones, like a new job or a relationship, or smaller things, like parking spaces and compliments. Making this list will give you reassurance and strengthen your beliefs that feeling it real works. Remember to feel grateful for each manifestation, because gratitude creates more reasons to feel grateful!